'DO SOMETHING ABOUT IT!'

'Do something about it!'
A MEDIA MAN'S STORY

BILL PORTER

Foreword by Gordon Graham
Afterword by Bernard Margueritte

Published 2005 by John Faber
2 Batworth Park House
Arundel, BN18 9PG, UK
johnfaber@tiscali.co.uk

ISBN 1 85239 036 0

In association with Caux Books
Rue du Panorama
1824 Caux, Switzerland

Copies are also available from the
International Communications Forum
24 Greencoat Place, London,
SW1P 1RD
icforum@yahoo.co.uk

Book design: Blair Cummock
Cover design: John Munro

Printed by Ashford Colour Press
Gosport, Hampshire, UK

To Natalie and Jabez,
my beloved granddaughter
and her Australian husband,
who together will help to make
the twenty first century
a time of greatness

So many people have helped me to get this book written, improved, designed and published, that I have to thank all of you in general rather than by name. Suffice it to say that most of you were my colleagues in the International Communications Forum, but also friends of my business and publishing life, those of my earlier years and members of my family.

Contents

Foreword

Bill Porter and I met as publishing competitors in the late 1970s. He had a tougher job than me, since he was managing director of a young company, while I was fortunate to be running the long entrenched market leader. This did not faze Bill, who combined innocent charm with shrewd judgment, and an air of gravitas. We became good friends, since we both believed that we should serve the industry of which we were part, in the course of serving our employers.

Shortly after we both attained our freedom from the discipline of the payroll, Bill wrote to me that he was planning to start something with the non-committal title of International Communications Forum (ICF) for the purpose of advocating better standards in the media, and he generously wondered if I would like to be associated with it. Both being ex-newspapermen who had turned to book publishing, who had travelled the world, and both lived for some years in India, we had a lot in common.

Although I did not join the mainstream of his initiative, I have been cheering him from the sidelines for the last fifteen years. I have attended some ICF meetings, and formed an admiration for the devotion of Bill and the group he gathered around him to the cause of improving the ethical standards of the media, particularly newspapers and television. During this period Bill and I have corresponded regularly (we are both old-fashioned letter-writers), and have met now and then. So I have been able through him to observe the inspiring growth of his idea.

Now he has written his autobiography, the third part of which deals with the ICF. Not one to shy away from fundamentals, Bill calls that part 'Destiny'. The first two parts are entitled 'Life', covering his childhood and professional career and 'Love', in which he tells with frankness, verging on painful honesty, the story of his marriage. Love is thus the central part of his book and its keynote. His late wife Sonja was the catalyst who moved him from the conventional life of the retired executive to his ICF adventure. 'Don't just complain. Do something,' she told him. Thus began a journey on which he has travelled cheerfully and optimistically with hundreds of like-minded companions.

Like many thoughtful octogenarians, Bill Porter is concerned about the future (see his dedication). He would like to leave more to the following generation than a memoir. Even so, his memoir, which forms the first part of the book, is a necessary framework for his message; it is not a bad yarn in its own right. But for Bill, it simply raises the curtain on what he sees as the meaning and purpose of his life.

Bill's story demonstrates the power of ideas. He did not retire rich, but he spent what he had on helping the idea along. The response has been such that he has organized, led and spoken at media conferences all over the world, arousing enthusiastic support from many media people, particularly the young from Eastern Europe and Asia, encouragement from readers and viewers, and at least respect from critics who regard him as an idealist remote from reality.

After he completed his manuscript, Bill recognized that it would not attain commercial publication. Publishing is a tough old world, and no one publishes out of friendship. Autobiographies are two a penny these days, and only those of the famous or scurrilous are offered contracts. Who wants to read about mere goodness these days? The answer is that many people do. Those who buy his book, whether Bill's constituents or those who discover him through the book, will not only be reading the credo of a remarkable man, but contributing to the cause to which he has devoted himself unreservedly for the past fifteen years.

GORDON GRAHAM
Marlow, May 2005

I

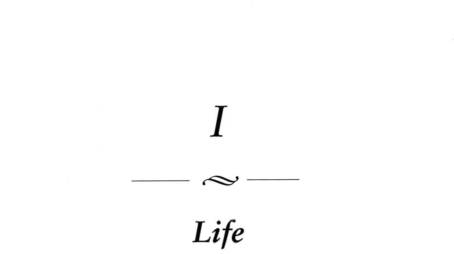

Life

Younger Days

I am told that, at the age of four, I was found in our kitchen garden joyfully eating freshly-pulled radishes, dirt and all. It's true that I have a liking for radishes to this day, especially the French way of *radis au beurre*. But many things I do remember from my childhood on a delightful farm called Falcons Hall, in the East Anglian county of Essex; the nearby seashore, the boisterous farm students and the arrival of a sister.

When I was five my father's pigs were infected with swine fever and had to be destroyed. There was no compensation for equipment or the loss of animals at that time and father had to sell at a low price. However he decided not to go bankrupt, but to use everything that he had to repay all his debtors. That left him with a wife and two children and another on the way with no means of livelihood. I learned later that he did this because he felt that it was the honest thing to do. That left an indelible mark on my mind.

Dad then became a village baker and postman, to enable us all to survive, in a little place called Wilstone in Hertfordshire. My major memory there is at the age of six leading all the boys in the village for a hike to climb a local hill called Ivinghoe. This would have been all very well, except that none of the anxious mums knew where we had gone and we were very late in returning. This episode did not make me a local hero, although it did perhaps reveal a potential for taking initiatives.

The major shadow of my boyhood was my father's illness and the restrictions that it placed on our family life, particularly my mother. As a result of a farm accident he became epileptic and experienced a noisy attack practically once a week. Mostly they occurred during the night, but sometimes at breakfast or supper and, occasionally, when we were visiting friends or attending an event. My mother's loyalty to him was exceptional. She must have dreamed of escaping from the burden of looking after him. But she was in love with him and he with her. Perhaps my sister and I were some compensation to her, because we were reasonably well behaved and did well at school.

They had met when she was managing her father's corn and provisions business and my father visited each week to buy grain and supplies for his parents' farm. Eventually they were married and set up on a farm in Essex at a village called Chapel, where I was born. So I have always been able to say that I was born in chapel, to the amusement of my nonconformist friends and, possibly the concern of my Catholic colleagues. I was always an avid reader and recall tackling quite hefty tomes at the age of six. But, as well as the more serious stuff, I much enjoyed the weekly comic papers published by D C Thomson of Dundee, a firm that exists to this day.

On Mondays there was *Adventure*, and then for other weekdays *Rover*, *Wizard*, and finally *Hotspur*. I noticed that Dad was a secret reader of them. I took on an evening paper round for the local newsagent for two or three years for which I was paid with free comics and Western stories. I was so gripped by the Westerns that, when in 2001 I attended a conference in Colorado, I felt that I knew the area from my boyhood reading.

The headmaster of our local primary school must have detected some literary inclinations in me, as he had me enter a national competition by the Royal Society for the Prevention of Cruelty to Animals to write an illustrated book on the care of pets. It was largely a scissors and paste job of cuttings and pictures from papers and magazines with a minimum of interposed text. But to my surprise and probably more so that of the headmaster, it won the national prize for children under 11 years old. I received a certificate and a beautiful book on animals, but I don't think that my work was ever published.

Much is made today of the desirability of the choice of school for children and of the importance of staying at the same school. But between the ages of five and 15 I went to five different schools with no more than four years at any one of them. I cannot remember any traumas. It just seemed to be natural to change schools as my parents moved around. By and large I enjoyed all of them, and my scholastic development was unaffected as I was top student at the end of it.

My middle name is Erasmus. Not very common for an English country boy. Apparently my grandfather, when he heard that my father was going to give me this name, travelled 200 miles – a long distance in those days – to try to prevent him from doing so. He claimed that it would give me lots of trouble at school and that the other boys would tease me unbearably. However my father was adamant. He was an admirer of the great scholar Erasmus of Rotterdam and must have, optimistically, had in his mind that, if I carried that name, some of his wisdom and scholarship might rub off on me.

My grandfather was right, because as soon as my school-mates learned of my second name, I received some ragging. The consequence was not so bad: it gave me a militant attitude. Anyone making fun of me was summoned to a fight behind the bike shed, and I must have been a good puncher because the name of Erasmus was rarely mentioned again. I was purely and simply Bill, because I did not care for Will, Willy or Billy. My wife cottoned on to this later in life and could usually bring me to heel by calling me Billy Boy, after the song *Where have you been all the day, my Billy Boy?*

Although I was a robust lad, I nevertheless suffered from an occasional sense of inner fear that I could not explain and still do not understand. When it struck me, I would find my mother, Grace, and cling to her until the feeling passed away. I also developed a fear of getting lockjaw. I must have read about it somewhere and it gave me a sense of horror. So much so that I would sometimes open and shut my jaws for some minutes to be sure that they were still working normally. I remember my relief when we were all inoculated at school against tetanus.

Perhaps many children suffer from these irrational fears and endure them as I did. I suppose it would be better if we could come out with them at the time and get a sympathetic hearing. Although they were a small part of an otherwise reasonably happy life, they did cast a shadow. Curiously enough, when I was recovering from the traumas of active service in the Second World War, I experienced that same sensation of inner fear and I would read for hours at night instead of sleeping, until it passed away. It was several years before it completely left me.

What happened to the old family ties? Across three generations my family changed from a close-knit group of caring people in the Fylde District of Lancashire, the hinterland of Blackpool, to a dispersed series of small units scattered across the world with little sense of belonging to one another. I can still remember as a small boy, on holiday with two of my aunties in seaside Thornton Clevelys, looking through the old photo albums picturing family outings to the hills or along rivers and the marking events of weddings and baptisms. They all exuded a sense of joy and togetherness, which was not being repeated in the events of my boyhood.

At some point in the Sixties my cousin David and I decided to organise a family reunion, perhaps out of a sense of trying to re-create the spirit of our earlier generations. We even put a deposit on a North Oxfordshire hotel that we thought would be attractive and central. Then between us we contacted all our family members, brothers and sisters, cousins, nephews and nieces, great aunts and uncles, grand-children and even some cousins twice removed. It was all to no avail. There was no wish to take part in any such event and we abandoned the effort and lost our deposit on the hotel. And yet, before World War II, the then senior people of our family had got together to save the reputation of an uncle who had unknowingly sold dud shares to the public. Instead of letting him go bankrupt they repaid all the people who had bought the shares. In another case they had contributed to an income for one of their womenfolk whose husband had been taken permanently ill.

Much of the change is due to the higher education of my grandparent's children. Most of the men took university degrees in medicine, science and agriculture. Some of the women qualified as teachers or married local men, who then left to make their careers elsewhere. There was an almost general exodus of that generation to careers and farms throughout Britain and, in some cases, to the British Common-wealth. In my teens the only close relatives left in the North Lancashire area were two aunts, one maiden and the other widowed, and two or three cousins twice removed.

The two World Wars and particularly the Second also played their part. Away from home our men and women fell in love with and married those who had no links with our home area. There was another and perhaps decisive influence, the coming of the so-called Welfare State with the concept of social security from the cradle to the grave. It was no longer necessary for families to look after their own, even in the well-to-do middle classes to which most of my relatives belonged. The more thinking and dynamic members of my generation held left-wing sympathies and were glad that the less fortunate members of our society would be better looked after and have access to health treatment, thanks to state provision.

In all fairness, lest you get the impression that my forbears were all sterling, unblemished citizens, I should tell the story of my paternal great-grandfather, a farmer, who took his produce for sale at Preston market once a week. Alas this became the opportunity for him to acquire a love of alcohol, and every market day he returned home completely drunk. His wife, who was a strong woman, did not take kindly to this and berated him fiercely on every occasion.

One market day, having already consumed a fair quantity of liquor, he thought that he could avoid the displeasure of his wife by bringing her the present of a beautiful set of crockery. And so, on his return, he offered it to her. She was not to be fooled and taking the crockery she smashed it to smithereens on the stone floor of the kitchen. This sobered him immediately and it is said that he broke down in tears and never touched a drop of alcohol again in his life. That led to a teetotal tradition in the family for three generations, alas, not followed by mine or succeeding generations. If my great-grandfather's experience for the cure of alcoholism were to be widely applied, there would be an awful of lot of smashed crockery around! Perhaps the suggestion should be labelled with every new tea or table set.

My parents told me that both of their families went back 400 years in the same district, which gave us very deep geographical roots. However, this never impressed me and I have had no wish to return there for my older days. So I was surprised on seeing a documentary about the Tartars, who had been displaced in Russia by Stalin and sent to distant parts, by their strong urge, when Communism collapsed, to return to the Crimea from whence they came. When asked why, they said because the bones of their ancestors were buried there. I could not for the life of me imagine wishing to return to Lancashire because the bones of my ancestors were in the local graveyards. I might have gone back for walks along the beach, to watch village cricket, for the local potted shrimps, for rides on the seafront trams, for sumptuous high teas, for the famous hot pot, for day trips to the Lake District and listening to tales told in the delightful district accent, and even to see the circus at Blackpool Tower, if some of those things still exist.

The game of cricket played an inescapable part in my youth. This is a game that has never been understood by the Latin countries and probably never will be. The idea of a game that lasts at least a good half-day, and in international contests can go on for five days, passes their comprehension. Nevertheless it has become *the* national sport in most parts of the old British Empire from Australia to the Caribbean, from Pakistan to South Africa.

During my Grammar School days there were two teams in the large village where I lived, one for the swanky, playing in the grounds of the local squire, and the other plebeian, playing on a roughly prepared pitch in the middle of a large field. Playing for both teams on different days I overcame the fear of a hard, seemingly huge ball smitten or bowled at me by tough young villagers. In my day it was hoped that this game would give us a sense of good sportsmanship, and teach us to lose with dignity and to win with humility.

What was the sum total of the family ethos that I took into manhood? It was a mixture of religious nonconformity, business acumen, professional success, and countryside ways of life. There was in it a sense of solidarity and kindness and a healthy respect for civilized behaviour.

As well as my sister, I also had a brother, John, who died as a baby, I think from what has become known as cot death, when I was only six years old. I was conscious of the deep sadness of my mother and father but probably, because I never knew him to play with and talk to, was not very affected. My sister was another matter. She was named Agnes after mother's twin sister, but for some reason did not like the name and later rechristened herself as Ann. She was of a robust and extrovert nature and followed me along by four years, as she still does. We had all the usual illnesses together, measles, chickenpox and mumps but she alone was afflicted with scarlet fever and went away to an isolation hospital for six weeks.

We were a united family, but not a close one. There was no lovie-doviness and we each guarded our own space and kept our own counsel. On balance that may have led to a stronger sense of independence and self-reliance. Just one of many good ways of growing up. As an aside to present-day youngsters, I walked two miles to primary school and later cycled nine miles to grammar school.

Eventually I went to Liverpool University with the help of an uncle and a small bursary and studied there from the year before World War II broke out until I was called up for military service. During my student years I sporadically sought after some kind of spiritual base, but this was usually backed into second place by my devotion to worldly success and pretty girls.

Wartime 1940-1946

At the beginning of my army service I was afraid of death, as were, almost certainly, most of us. One heard of people without fear and I assumed that they must be mentally unbalanced. It was apparent, nevertheless, that some overcame their fear at the point of combat. Was it because of patriotism, a sense of duty, fear of the scorn of comrades, of punishment or what?

I can never remember it being a subject of open discussion. We kept our fears to ourselves. During the days before embarking on a troopship headed for North Africa, I was stewing on this subject. Then for some reason I decided, 'OK, I am going to die. So, just accept that and forget about it.' And that was what happened. In accepting death, I lost my fear of it. In spite of a number of close calls, I was never in the grip of that particular fear again. In some ways courting with death was a fascination. I was not an infantryman. They would know when they were going to face death. But I was a signalman in an infantry division and, when in action, we were constantly subject to mortar and artillery fire. You could hear it coming, except for the high velocity shells. It must have been the same with bombs in the cities at home.

Once I went back for a visit to Liverpool, where I had been a student, and discovered that the building where I had lodgings had been flattened to the ground. If I had not been called up, I might have been dead! It was just opposite the Anglican Cathedral, which survived the war with a few scars.

I later saw the great spire of Cologne Cathedral still standing in the midst of ruins. Were church buildings always spared? Was there some kind of divine protection? Of course not. The Guards Chapel in London was hit by a flying bomb during a service with great loss of life and destruction.

Much later in life I was sometimes asked if I had a specific Church connection. Which always reminded me of when I was being checked into the Army by a sergeant who asked me what my religion was. I hesitated and the sergeant said, 'All right then, Church of England. And you'll thank me for that when on Sundays, instead of peeling potatoes in the cookhouse, you can go on Church parade.' On such a low level of conviction I became an Anglican. In a way I suppose that the sergeant was right, because Anglicanism is the state religion and we are, presumably, of that persuasion unless we profess something else or consciously opt out.

My army life followed the usual pattern of drill, marching, arms training with rifles and Bren guns, then promotion to lance corporal, where my principal task was to look after the unit's mail. After selection for training to be an officer at Catterick Camp in North Yorkshire I was commissioned as a second lieutenant, becoming a full lieutenant after six months with a line of communications signals unit preparing to join the First Army in Algeria. In 1942 came the day when we received our marching orders and assembled on the Glasgow docks to board a troopship with the New Zealand name of the *Aorangi*.

It was then that I had my first experience of the importance of industrial relations or, in this case, the lack of them, because the dockworkers went on strike and we had to load our stores and equipment ourselves. We were not very good at it, but somehow we managed, whilst being very critical that dockers could go on strike in wartime when we were preparing to risk our lives, first of all on the high seas and then against Rommel's German army. Although as a student I had considered joining the International Brigade in the Spanish Civil War and was an ardent reader of the Left Book Club published by

Victor Gollancz, I was disturbed by the kind of politics behind such industrial action.

Our convoy steamed and dieselled into the Atlantic and for several weeks we manoeuvred to avoid the U-boats, but, apart from our ship being cautioned for giving off too much black smoke with the risk of drawing our position to the attention of a surface raider, we eventually passed through the Straits of Gibraltar and landed without incident in the port of Algiers.

There were a few mishaps during the unloading, including seeing a lorry driver swing his three-ton truck alongside the dock and so close to the edge that when he stepped out of his cabin he fell straight into the water and we had to fish him out. And I gasped when I saw an officer's tin trunk fall from a crane's lifting net at a considerable height and concertina on to the concrete dock floor. Happily it was not mine!

We spent a few days camped out in the Forêt de Ferdinand on the city outskirts and then formed up into a section convoy with eight three-ton lorries, four 15-hundred-weight trucks, a jeep and half a dozen motor bikes ready for the long journey to Tunisia, where fighting had only recently ended.

In 1943, the German and Italian armies in North Africa had finally surrendered. Our 40 or so men had to find places for themselves as best they could in the backs of the lorries amongst our equipment. The most comfortable job was to be a driver, but they were inexperienced on rough and mountainous roads and crashed two of our vehicles into steep ditches and had to be abandoned, causing even greater overcrowding in the remaining transport. On arrival at the port of Bizerte I checked in with two drivers at the Ordnance Park and immediately, without question, took delivery of two replacement trucks. There was no red tape in war zones!

We hung around in Tunisia for some weeks whilst the American and British armies invaded and occupied Sicily and moved into the Italian mainland. Then it was our turn and we boarded a vehicle-carrying landing ship that rolled horribly during the crossing, en-route as it turned out for somewhere in the Salerno and Naples area. It was an American-crewed ship and at first my men enjoyed the strong tasty coffee, but, when they discovered that there was no tea onboard, morale slumped badly. After three days at sea they were eager to make the landing, if only to be able to brew tea again. Danger seemed to fade into a lesser concern!

We were ordered to move across Italy to the city of Bari on the Adriatic Sea and were stationed a few miles to the south in a small port. Shortly after we arrived the German Air Force very successfully bombed Bari harbour, sinking many ships and damaging the installations. A big failure had been the communications system leading to a lack of co-ordination of the air defences. Our first job was to repair the existing system and to add new links, including a buried multi-channel cable. I was given a section from the Italian army, which had come over to the Allied side, consisting of a very short but pompous lieutenant and about 20 men, to do the digging and the hard work. One day they did not turn up and I contacted the officer. '*Oggi e festa*,' he told me (today is a feast day). 'All right', I said, 'then you'll be back to work tomorrow.' 'Oh no,' he said, *Domani è dopodomani è anche festa* (tomorrow and the day after are feast days as well). It was a new one to me that the war could be put aside for feast days, no matter how holy they might be.

I was getting bored with working in the rear echelons and asked for a transfer to a front-line unit. This was granted and my driver-batman drove me northwards from Bari via Naples and Rome to catch up with the 78th British Infantry Division, at that time just over the high summits of the Appenines between Florence and Bologna. We came into Florence where all the bridges had been blown down by the retreating Germans, with the exception of the irreplaceable Ponte Vecchia. The German commander did not have the heart to destroy such a world heritage and instead blew up the buildings at each end, so effectively blocking it to vehicles, but preserving the bridge.

The Italians have said that many of the great art treasures of their country disappeared during, and shortly after, the war. I can well believe this, as many opportunities for temptation must have arisen. Coming into Florence I had my own experience of this when we drew up for a few minutes outside a large building. I walked inside, as no one was looking after it, and wandered into the cellars. On the floor in rows around the walls were a great number of paintings. I drew one of them back to look at and I was sure that it was the painting of Saint Francis by Titian.

I am no art expert, but it seemed to me that many famous paintings from buildings in Florence had been rapidly stored there to protect them from the fighting. It only occurred to me later that I could easily have cut several canvases from their frames and kept them as trophies of war to be sold at a later, convenient date. I imagine that some, less scrupulous than I, took advantage of such opportunities.

That night I stayed at a commandeered hotel used for officers in-transit and had dinner with an infantry officer taking a break from the line. He asked me what job I was going to and, when I said to be a brigade signals officer, he said, 'Then your life expectancy is only a few weeks, so you had better get drunk and find a woman, because it will be your last chance.' Happily I did not follow his advice and instead had a hot bath and a good sleep.

However, on awakening early the next morning, the purport of his remarks bore in on me strongly. I got dressed and wandered about the streets and, by chance, came to Florence's great-domed cathedral. I went in and prayed, for the first time in many years, largely in the hope of God giving me rather longer than a few weeks. At least in my case that seems to have worked! Nor did the job turn out to be as risky as all that, apart from dodging plenty of shell bursts.

We were stuck on those mountains during a very cold winter and our division was allocated to the American Fifth Army with General Mark Clark in command. I saw him once or twice bowling by in his jeep, displaying his athletic and smartly dressed figure. I was mystified as to why we had so many US 'liaison' officers visiting our mess around meal times and hoping to be offered a meal. It turned out to be due to the American feeding policy based on canned and preserved food, whereas the British aimed to buy as much fresh food as possible as they moved through the countryside and, consequently, it was much more appetising. No wonder we were an attraction to our Allies who didn't get a decent cooked meal in months.

I remember a certain length of road in the Italian Appenines between Florence and Bologna, which connected our Main and Rear Division Headquarters and which was constantly under shellfire. We would tear down that road in a jeep or truck, hoping not to be hit, and getting a tremendous kick when we got safely to the other end. I am sure that some of us did it just to get the kick.

What was not so good was getting fired at by your own planes, which sometimes happened in fast moving warfare. If that occurred when we were on the road, we ran our vehicles into the hedges and ditches and leapt out, hopefully, to safety, then cursing and swearing as we saw the disappearing tail of an RAF fighter. Fortunately it was a rare occurrence; there is nothing worse than to be killed or wounded by your own so-called 'friendly' fire.

My immediate superior officer was Captain Michael Stanley, son of the War Minister. He was something of a radio expert, highly independent, and very bright, but sadly afflicted with a pronounced stutter. We had met before as private soldiers at a Pre-Officer Training Unit where he had a maverick reputation. On one occasion he was in charge of the night guard, when the orderly officer called in at the gate hut to find no one there. So he waited and, after a while there was the clip clop of the guard, six men and Stanley, marching back to their post. When angrily confronted with his dereliction of duty, unabashed, Stanley stuttered, 'Ww-w-w-well, sir, it is a v-very hot n-n-night, so I thought I'd m-m-march 'em off to the l-local pub for a d-drink.' Doubtless, due to his family connections he got away with it.

On another occasion, on pay parade, his turn came to go to the paying-out major to receive a pittance of about ten shillings at the time. The drill was to march smartly up to the table, salute, accept the pay packet, salute, turn round and smartly march away. Stanley must have slouched up, because the major rebuked him for sloppiness and told him to go out and try again. The second effort was not much better, if at all, and, once more the major told him to do it again. Then Stanley, for whom ten shillings was not a great attraction, said, 'Alright then, you can k-keep your b-blooming pay,' and abruptly left the room. Being who he was he was quietly handed his pay privately later in the day.

Back in the Italian mountains, Christmas 1944 was nearing and Stanley decided that he would give our section a treat and sent the water truck down to Florence where he paid to have it filled with wine. It was a 40-mile journey in each direction over tank-rutted and uneven mountain roads, but eventually the truck arrived to a thirsty welcome by us all in eager anticipation. Stanley poured out the first mugful, took a mouthful and then spat it out in complete disgust. It was undrinkable. The driver had forgotten to remove the filtration unit which purified the water and several hundred litres of wine had been chlorinated during the bumpy journey. Stanley was almost apoplectic with rage and expressed himself with a fine collection of stuttered English expletives.

I did not keep in touch with him after the war, but on one occasion we bumped into one another at Kings Cross Station in London. I had read somewhere that he had become the Chief Executive of a major company, which had aroused my curiosity.

So I questioned him as to how he achieved this eminence. Still stuttering, but admirably self-deprecatory he said, 'Oh, it was easy. I m-m-married the ch-chairman's daughter.'

The Polish Corps were on our right and they were highly effective soldiers. But it was the time of the Yalta Agreement between Roosevelt and Stalin when they carved up post-war Europe between them, with Poland remaining within the Russian sphere of influence. This was a deadly blow to the Poles, who felt that they had been betrayed, and so they had. The Corps remained loyal to their military commitments, but to a man they went into mourning, not even accepting their drinks, cigarettes and chocolate rations. How the Allied leaders overcame their embarrassment I do not know.

Came the Spring of 1945 with the last great offensive in Northern Italy, when we swept across the Po Valley, leaving fields full of prisoners of war and on into the foothills of the Alps. Such was our efficiency by that time that a whole division was moving, tanks and all, at getting on for 200 miles a day. When we were on the edge of running out of petrol, there would always be a stockpile of jerry-cans brought up by the Ordnance Corps, where we could fill up and be off again within minutes.

Our crossing-place into Austria was the Monte Croce Pass and I remember the thrill of reaching the top between high cliffs of rock and then zooming down into the Drau River valley and Carinthia, where we immediately established Allied Occupation authority. Perhaps, more than anywhere else in Europe, this area had been untouched by the rigours and hardships of war. Everyone seemed to be comfortable and well fed, but neither did we speak the language nor understand what might be going on in the hearts and minds of the people. Our occupation location was on the shores of the Milstadtersee, a beautiful, fish-filled lake. I had picked up an amphibian Volkswagen and tested it out by crossing the lake without capsizing.

Now we had to become serious occupiers and I remember

billeting my men in private houses by the process of knocking on doors and saying, *Haben sie ein Schlafzimmer fur zwei Soldaten?* and the answer had to be *Ja*! I found a very nice home for myself with a rich businessman, who seemed to have led a prosperous and comfortable war. The only problem was that he had two beautiful daughters and the army had a policy of non-fraternisation with the local people. I managed to survive unscathed.

By a stroke of luck I became very popular with the local occupying troops, as I was given the welfare task of getting the nearby brewery in Spittal going again. This I managed to do, in spite of zero knowledge of the brewing art, because the workers were keen anyway on drinking their own product again. The beer was of a natural quality that would have gladdened the heart of any real ale enthusiast. Military morale was given a definite boost both in the soldiers' canteens and the officers' messes.

Here my division had one of its hardest and saddest tasks of the whole war. Part of the Yalta Agreement was that all Russian troops, especially those who had collaborated with the enemy should be returned to Russian hands and vice versa with Allied troops. So-called White Russians and disillusioned prisoners of war were recruited into service divisions by the Germans. They were not combat divisions and, in many cases, soldiers' families moved with the troops. We had overrun some such forces and were obliged by the Agreement to hand them over. This happened at a particular point by loading them into trains, which were then driven across into the Russian Zone. In the process many White Russians committed suicide and others were forced onto the trucks by our men at the point of the bayonet. The women and children were wailing in grief and terror. Many of our battle-hardened soldiers said that this was their worst experience of the whole war. Eye witnesses told us that as soon as the White Russians were unloaded from the rail wagons, any of them identified as officers were shot on the spot and the rest herded into waiting trains, sent on the long journey to slave labour camps in Siberia and never seen again.

An event even more notorious was to follow. Quite a lot of Yugoslav resistance troops from both the Tito forces and from royalist and non-Communist groups were roaming around in Carinthia. The Tito elements even put up posters saying that they were the occupation force in the area and should be obeyed by the populace. The British army reacted to this by putting up posters saying that if all Yugoslavs had not handed in their arms by a certain time they would be shot at. It had the required effect, but it must have been difficult for the British to distinguish between the different loyalties of the Yugoslavs, although Tito's men usually had a red star on their uniform.

I later read that we had persuaded the non-Communists to board trains on the understanding that they were going to Italy, but in fact the trains were driven into Northern Yugoslavia and into the hands of Tito's forces. It is thought that most of them were slaughtered as traitors and buried in huge graves. There is much controversy about this incident and Nikolai Tolstoy, grandson of the great writer, suffered badly from writing a book on the subject, criticising the British authorities.

The pleasures of occupation life in Austria were not to last long for me. The war was still going on in Asia and the Japanese army had to be dislodged from most of SouthEast Asia and Indonesia. I was quickly transferred to an Indian Army brigade, given six weeks leave in England and shipped off to India. Thus began my lifetime love of the Indian sub-continent and its peoples and cultures. Our Brigade, 17th Indian Infantry, was stationed in the jungles in Central India to the south of an army town called Saugor.

We were being trained as an air-transported force for the invasion of Sumatra, the major Indonesian island. There was supposed to be some similarity between the Indian jungle terrain and that of our destination. We spent a lot of time getting in and out of old Dakota plane bodies, as this type of plane and towed gliders were to be our means of transport across the Indian Ocean. It would be a one-way trip to crash landings on the Sumatran beaches and a warm welcome by stubborn and ruthless Japanese soldiers. No one was looking forward to the experience.

I rather enjoyed being the Brigade Signals Officer, as I had an excellent and varied group of men. Some of them were Dogras, who had typical pointed moustaches. You could always tell the state of their morale, because, when it was low, the moustaches drooped. We had Hindus, Moslems and Christians, the main advantage of which was that we all celebrated all the Holy days without any friction and usually with much enjoyment, particularly if a feast was involved.

One night as I slept in my tent, a troop of large monkeys swung through the jungle and took my tent as just another tree to swing by. My tent folded around me, and monkey after monkey landed on my back in passing, leaving me very battered and the contents of the tent very flattened. Another animal incident occurred when I was driving along a dusty road at full speed in my jeep, when an old cow began to slowly cross the road about 50 yards ahead. I had been well informed that to Hindus the cow was a sacred animal and that any British soldier who killed one would be severely punished. So I applied the brakes with great vigour, went into enormous swerves, almost lost control and finally came to rest giving the cow a gentle push in the stomach. It turned and looked at me with much disdain and, at the same slow pace, completed its crossing of the road. I came to the conclusion that, in the course of many generations it must have been bred into the cows that they had nothing to fear from mankind.

The suspense of oncoming danger was suddenly lifted to the immense relief of all. Atomic bombs had been dropped on

Hiroshima and Nagasaki and the Japanese had unconditionally surrendered. The bombs had dropped, so we would not. We had no idea of the significance of what had happened, of the dangers of an atomic age, of the possibility that all human life could be wiped out and that it would lead to an arms race between two power blocks on a scale never known in history. No, we just slept better that night and the next day our thoughts turned to an early home going.

Some years later I realised that during all my life in the army, as a private soldier and as a junior officer, I never knew what was going on further away from me than a few hundred yards and I certainly did not know why anything was happening. Consequently after demobilisation, I bought all the books that I could find on the Italian Campaign, written by journalists and generals, to enlighten my ignorance. It was the writing of the enemy commanders that I found to be the most interesting, as it told us how we could have shortened the war if our commanders had done this instead of that. But I learned a great deal from the other books as well, especially about trying to understand the whole picture in any given situation.

Post-war Idealism

Following my return to civilian life, I resumed my studies at Liverpool University, but without interest in the subject. An uncle of mine had persuaded the editor of his regional daily to take me on as a junior reporter, but before starting I had arranged a transfer to Leeds University to take a degree in Social Science, which I could complete in two years.

In the meantime I was approached by some of the Moral Re-Armament (MRA) people whom I had briefly met in Italy, one of them being a distant cousin, Ronald Mann, who had been taken prisoner, escaped and walked his way back to the Allied lines along the Appenine Mountains. Somehow they persuaded me to join them in MRA's post-war activities and to use such journalistic talents as I might have in editing their news service, writing press releases and taking part in their programme of improving industrial relations in the crisis areas of Western Europe. Those turned out to be the British coal-fields and the textile factories of France interspersed with periodic stays in London, Paris and Geneva.

What I had expected to be a temporary move eventually extended into the mid-Fifties, encouraged by my meeting and then close association with a remarkable Frenchman called Maurice Mercier. During the war he had been part of the Communist-led resistance movement, but became disillusioned with Communist policies and helped to form the democratic trade union movement *Force Ouvrière*. As a Marxist he had believed that, as the structures of society changed, so the nature of man would be bettered, but he quickly grasped that

the MRA idea of creating a new type of man, who was motivated by honesty and unselfishness, would be better able to
build a just society. He understood that such a group of men
and women would be a guiding influence that could redirect
the dangerous missiles of hate-directed Communism and
greed-directed capitalism, for the benefit of all humanity. His
vision, his intellect and his commitment certainly inspired me
and I had the privilege of accompanying him on some of his
trade union visits across France and also on journeys to the
USA and India.

What struck me with Mercier was that at a time when so
many other Communists abandoned their faith in the ideology
that had been their whole purpose in life, he found another
form of militant action that allowed him to pursue his ideal.
He often told me that he had found in Moral Re-Armament a
more complete and satisfying revolution than Communism.
Mercier played a key part in stabilizing the French textile
industry and in bringing about its post-war recovery.

I can remember walking with him for miles along Paris
streets, *flâner* as they called it, and being amazed at his ency-
clopaedic knowledge of the lives and histories of the street
names. He was certainly the best-read trade union leader, or
businessman for that matter, that I ever met. Although our
ways parted, my friendship with Maurice lasted until his
death.

For several summers I was a press correspondent in Geneva,
following the conferences of the International Labour Organisation and the United Nations Economic and Social Council, for
the International Labour News Service, which had been set up
by an MRA-motivated Scottish journalist called Tom Gillespie.
Tom eventually married his boyhood sweetheart and emigrated
to Australia where he lives to this day, staying in an elderly
people's home, but still battling to challenge his beloved newspaper world, through letters and phone calls to his many
contacts in journalism and broadcasting, to be a force for good.

Whilst in Geneva along with another colleague, David Hind, who later became marketing director of a leading British printing company, we invited business, labour and political leaders to take part in the weekend Industrial Conferences at the MRA Centre at Caux, high on the mountainside above Montreux at the other end of Lake Geneva. We must have been pretty persuasive, because sometimes we had to hire a coach to take them all there. It was to be 35 years later that I set foot in Caux again.

* * * * * * *

If I put the various times together, I must have lived in India for some five years of my life. It is almost certainly the country that has had the deepest influence on me. My first experience of the sub-continent had been those six months in the Indian Army during the winter of 1945 to 46. Then for four years from 1955 to 59, working with Moral Re-Armament, editing a newsletter. I also wrote freelance for newspapers and magazines including *The Scotsman* of Edinburgh, the *Indian Express* of New Delhi, and other Indian dailies; in the UK the *City Press*, the *Contemporary Review*, and the *New Strand* of London; the International Labor News Service of the USA and other articles and radio broadcasts. Nehru was then at the height of his powers. On the economic side, the Five-Year Plans were bringing industrialisation and irrigation across the land.

It was also when, for the first time, a Communist government was elected democratically in State elections, in Kerala, the southernmost part of western India. It was the most highly educated region. When I went down there I found, for example, that of more than 400 applicants for bus conductors' jobs in Trivandrum's municipal service, some 200 had university degrees. That highlighted the major problem, unemployment, certainly a prime reason for the voting result. Amazingly, having been voted in, there was a rapid turn of opinion to hostility. At one point thousands of women dressed in white made a silent march of protest, passing before the Parliament. Eventually the state of unrest became so great that the Indian Government stepped in and declared Central rule, appointing a Governor to do the job of running the State until the next elections, when the Congress Party returned to power.

Other memories of Kerala are the tall coconut palms sweeping down to the edge of the ocean, of the steep drop of the beach only a few metres from the shore, of sleeping in the unmarried quarters of the State Parliament and of, surprisingly, meeting a Ugandan Prince studying medicine in the university.

The most common car in India was the Hindustan Ambassador, being a locally manufactured version of an earlier Austin-Morris model. Driving one brought me into contact with the amazing life of the Indian roads. For the most part they consisted of a macadamised central track, rarely wide enough for two vehicles and with bumpy, dusty borders into which one ventured when overtaking or avoiding an oncoming vehicle. The enormous population of the country was illustrated when one stopped along the road for comfort or a snack. From nowhere would appear children and old people to gaze with curiosity and possibly entertainment at us travellers from what must have seemed another world, wearing our extraordinary clothing and eating our unusual dishes.

Road incidents included driving across a swollen river where the bridge had been swept away and replaced with rocks and branches. We must have been crazy to try to attempt it. Halfway across I was sure that we would be swept into the torrent and end up as a pile of scrap iron further downstream. Fate was with us and we made it, but it must have been an hour before my colleague and I felt sufficiently relaxed to talk again.

I discovered that it was possible to suffer food poisoning, and feel much better for it. Today one can take a rather expensive two-day course to completely empty the digestive system, removing all traces of undigested material with apparently health-giving results. Indian poisonings did that for me without charge. I often felt so exhilarated afterwards, that I could be looking forward to the next similar experience!

In the early days of the Indian Parliament, in a rush of unthought-through but idealistic legislation, a law changing driving on the left to driving on the right, was proposed. It quickly turned out to be impracticable, as all the many animals using the road – buffaloes, cattle, ponies, horses and camels – were firmly used to being on the left, and they did not grasp any change in the regulations. The law was abandoned and India drives on the left to this day.

Another well-intentioned piece of planned legislation that came to grief was that of raising the school leaving age to 15 within five years, when it was realised that it would take 20 years to train enough teachers to be able to do it.

When I first arrived in India I was very self-assured and felt able to diagnose and write about any subject with great certainty. When I left India four years later, I realised that I knew very little, having been faced with a 4,000-year-old civilisation and a deep spirituality beyond my comprehension. I had also been arrogant enough to think that many Indian beliefs and customs were ridiculous and intellectually indefensible.

One enlightening experience stands out. I became quite friendly with the Chief Secretary of the Ministry of Finance. He had a powerful and analytical mind and was coping with the vast problems of the Indian economy with much success. But he told me that he had a guru, who always knew what he was doing and whose advice he always accepted. 'For example,' he said, 'when I fly on Ministry business and meet my guru on return he tells me that I had been to Bombay or wherever and met such and such a person, even though I had never informed him.' Now my western mind told me that this was nonsense and the guru could not possibly have known these things. But my friend believed in it, and I believed in him, so I had to accept it. This for me was the beginning of an understanding and appreciation of the beliefs of others.

In Benares, now called Varanasi, the holy city on the Ganges, bordered by temples and bathing places, I stayed for a week or two as the guest of an engineer responsible for the safe upkeep of the river banks. Any collapse could have risked the lives of hundreds of people worshipping and praying. There were some amazing sights of devotion to Krishna and the deistic panoply. One man had put his arm straight up in the air for many years and it had become immovable in that position. Another followed the sun with his eyes from dawn to sunset and had become completely blind. Several enormously fat holy men did nothing but eat the sweets that pilgrims bought for them. The pilgrims also gave money for the maintenance of their temple.

In the home of the engineer, I noticed that he was subscribed to both *Time* magazine and *The Economist*, but, without reading them, he put them away in his attic. Eventually, overcome with curiosity at this dismissive way of handling the news, I asked him what he was doing. 'Oh,' he said, 'I intend to read them when I retire, going backwards from the latest issue to those I first bought.' Well, there's no accounting for taste and I don't suppose that the circulation managers of those two publications would be worried. He was also a palmist and, having read my palm, informed me that I was headed for a long life and an interesting marriage. It looks as though he was not far wrong.

Most Indians and nearly all Sri Lankans that I met believed in the importance of astrology. Personally, I didn't then and I don't now. But I hope that I have made it clear that what I do or do not believe is a subjective matter of small importance in the scheme of things. How I live and behave is another matter with wider implications! Many friends I knew would not travel until they had consulted their astrologer and most government decisions in Sri Lanka were taken with astrologers' advice.

There came a time when I was a guest at a Hindu wedding. Now these can be two-day affairs, and the crucial moment in the ceremony, after which there can be no turning back, is fixed by an astrologer. My friend told me that his bride's father's astrologer had first fixed this time for four o'clock in the morning, which was thought to be very inconvenient. His father-in-law then gave some more rupees to the astrologer and told him to try again. That brought it round to two o'clock, which was still not good enough. Eventually, by virtue of further payments and further zodiacal researches, it was finalised at ten in the evening.

I note that most of today's western popular papers have astrology columns, and I therefore assume that they are read by millions of people. I have myself read them to get the drift. To me they come through as well-intentioned advice and recommendations, which could hardly cause harm and might even do occasional good. For example, 'Try to see your mother-in-law in a more friendly light.' 'Be alert for a good business opportunity this afternoon.' 'Your natural wit should hold you in good stead during a trying period.' They don't go quite as far as the old Cornish saying that, 'It is very unlucky to drop a £20 note in the fire on Tuesdays.'

Travelling by train is a great feature of Indian life. It is so popular that in third class compartments there are usually about three times as many people as there are seats. This produces a three-layer arrangement – one on the floor, another on the seats and a third on the luggage racks. Quite ingenious in its way and, fortunately, not smelly, as the Indians keep very clean. Much more so than excited football crowds in the North of England.

Coming back by train from an event far from Delhi, I found that some people had arrived a day early at the station and the majority were there several hours ahead of departure time. Recalling that I once had a friend who believed in catching trains as they were just moving out of the station, because it was a tremendous waste of time hanging around on platforms, I made enquiries of fellow travellers as to why they came so soon. Firstly, it gives the opportunity to meet people and to chat; secondly, there is a wider range of refreshments than back in the town; thirdly, you sleep more comfortably on the platform than in the train; fourthly, the pan, a mild chewing drug, is better at the stations and fifthly, there are lots of people to play cards with and to compete in various trials of strength. I was inveigled into arm wrestling when you put your elbows on the table, clasp wrists and try to bend the other down until his hand touches the table. I had a sore arm for a fortnight after that.

Whilst living in India I was able to visit East Pakistan, which is now Bangladesh, and Sri Lanka. At that time, there were only minor restrictions to travel. It was said of Ernest Bevin, Britain's war-time and immediate post-war Foreign Minister that he had defined his foreign policy to enable people to go to the railway station and buy a ticket to anywhere in the world without needing visas and with no conditions. How far we still are from such a goal! In Pakistan a close friend, Bill Cockburn, who had been an Edinburgh trade union activist, and I had a meeting with the military dictator, General Ayub Khan, a species to which the Pakistanis are now well accus tomed. He met us at his residence at Murree, a Himalayan hill station, and took us for a long walk, fortunately along the flat, unaccompanied by guards and security men, hardly possible in later years, when no one is safe from terrorist attacks at any place or at any time, or from assassinations if you are a figurehead.

Later, on the same trip, we visited Peshawar and travelled up the Khyber Pass to set foot in Afghanistan. This is traditional gun country and there are some villages where they

make replicas of army rifles that are as accurate as the origi-
nals. Most men travel around with a gun slung over their
shoulders. When eating in Peshawar restaurants we saw diners
place their rifles on top of the table to reassure everyone that
no shooting was going to take place during mealtimes. I could-
n't help thinking of the comparison with the distinguished and
extravagant restaurants of Paris, where the worst that one
might fear would be a plate of soup misdirected onto one's lap.

In Bangladesh I flew up to the tea-growing area around
Sylhet in an old Dakota largely used for transporting tea to
Dacca, the capital, and onward transmission. The system for
passengers was that you removed enough tea chests to put in
seats for the human requirements, often rather grudgingly
conceded.

Why did I walk out from the MRA scene? There was an
ideological reason and a case might be made for it. Back in
France, before I left for India, I'd seen through Maurice
Mercier what could have become a mass movement for higher
moral values seeming to take shape. He and some leading
French business and political leaders under the MRA banner
had filled the great Sports Centre in Lille and the Salle de la
Mutualité in Paris with enthusiastic crowds. They were aiming
to do the same at the vast Vélodrome d'Hiver, which only the
Communists had been able to fill with, I recall, some 20,000
people.

I had been gripped by the potential of this situation and
Mercier felt that we could raise the level of responsible citizen-
ship by at least ten per cent if we got the ball rolling. At this
point we came up against the view of the prevailing MRA
leadership that it was more important to have ten totally
committed people to their ideals rather than an unquantifiable
and perhaps marginal improvement in general behaviour. The
mass movement idea was halted in its tracks and I started to
lose interest in the, at-the-time, narrower objectives of the
MRA people. I had accepted the invitation to go to India, still

under the aegis of MRA, but with the intention of returning to a career in journalism. I eventually flew from Bombay back to Europe and began the tough experience of establishing my life in the commercial world of writing and publishing. In all fairness, I should also mention that I found the strict attitude of MRA towards relationships with the female sex very restricting, and I was looking forward to my freedom in that respect.

During my time with the people of MRA I sincerely tried to find a faith, even to become a Christian, but deep in my mind I remained an agnostic. But I had a real admiration for their sincerity and basic goodness. I rejected the lies and misinterpretation of them made by a warped minority of my colleagues in the media. I admired the courageous efforts of one of Britain's finest journalists, Peter Howard, to present the truth about the MRA people and their fight for moral values in the highest circles of British and international life. But I didn't accept his personal challenge. I still remember him saying, 'You are meant to be a mighty tree, under whose branches many people can find shelter and purpose,' but I didn't grasp his vision for me.

I had no more contact with him, and he died of an acute illness during a major campaign in South America many years later. I have since renewed contact with his widow, Doë, now a vibrant, alert woman in her nineties, and she has helped me to feel that I have tried to pick up the baton which fell from Howard's hands in his fight for a positive media.

Bookselling – a Life on the Road

When I came back from India to England, for two or three years I made a modest living as a freelance journalist. But then, by an unexpected chance, I left the world of writing myself for that of getting others to write, due to the death of my Uncle Jack Porter. He had been a leading agricultural adviser and farming author, who named his house Cromhampstone, inspired by his political heroes Cromwell, Hampden and Gladstone. I had liked him without admiring him. When driving his car he had the habit of talking to it as though it were a horse that he was coaxing over the jumps. He was a local councillor and played for the village cricket team well into his sixties, though I never saw him score a run or take a wicket. Two of the books he wrote, *The Cropgrower's Companion* and *The Stockfeeder's Companion*, had been a boon to farmers of an earlier generation.

Of course I went to his funeral and, walking in the cortege behind the coffin, I was beside a man of about my age whom I had never met before. He asked me what I was doing and I explained that I had just returned from abroad and was looking for work as a journalist. He asked me if I had ever thought of book publishing. I replied not particularly, but that I was ready for anything. The upshot was that he invited me to lunch at the Royal Automobile Club in London's Pall Mall for the following Tuesday and over coffee offered me a job in his publishing company. It was just beside the Law Courts and near to the famous Fleet Street, where at that time most of our national daily newspapers were published. I was thrilled by the location and highly relieved to be earning a steady salary, as getting established in journalism after a lengthy period abroad was a precarious business.

My boss was John Grant from a celebrated Edinburgh family that owned antiquarian bookshops and a modern educational publishing house. He had decided to leave the family firms and to make his own way. This he did by joining the famous Oxford booksellers, Blackwell, rising up through the ranks and then setting up Blackwells Scientific, which became an important imprint in that subject area. When I joined him he ran a publishing consultancy practice and was beginning a new management book imprint.

One of the first tasks that I was given was to proofread a *Directory of British Scientists*, an exceptionally boring activity involving checking the print proofs with the original text and correcting any literals, errors arising in the typesetting process. Our book had to be cleared by Government security to be sure that we were not disclosing information about the scientists listed that would be helpful to Britain's enemies, at that time the Soviet Union. Even so, when I visited Moscow some months later, I managed to sell 200 copies to their Import/Export Book Company.

Another duty was to bring suitable British titles to the attention of a number of United States and Canadian publisher clients, which they might like to import in sufficient quantities to have the exclusive selling rights in the USA and traditional territories. This latter work eventually led to my taking a business trip to North America to liaise with our existing clients, and to seek new ones. One of our publishers was Richard D Irwin, one of the world's best business management educational imprints. We had been doing so well for their European sales that we had received a telex telling us to slow down as we were causing them 'serious inventory problems' back at Homewood, Illinois, an outer suburb of Chicago. We framed that telex for display in our office. Their Sales Director, John Ecob, looked after me during my visit and at one point I suggested that he visit Europe to better understand the market there. 'Come over to Europe!' he said, 'I haven't even been into the centre of Chicago for the last six months.' This was an early experience for me of an unexpected United States insularity or perhaps it should be called continentalarity.

I much enjoyed a visit in Canada to the University of Toronto Press to meet its internationally respected director, Marsh Jeanneret. He had a private island on Lake Muskoga, to the north of the metropolis, and invited me there for a weekend. We crossed to it in a top-grade motorboat in which he speeded us around the lake until we berthed at his island holiday lair. My principal memory of the stay is of diving into the water, which was covered with pollen, and emerging looking like a green man from Mars. I also learned much in listening to the wisdom of a world leader in scholarly publishing.

I attended the American Booksellers Association's annual convention at which nearly all American publishers had a stand, although at that time the British and the rest of the world were not much in evidence, with the exception of the highly successful Paul Hamlyn, who had an amazing flair for selecting and selling popular titles. He told me that we were the only British there and that this was a national disgrace. Of course I was glad to be on the side of the angels, albeit somewhat overawed that the great man had condescended to talk to me. Strangely our paths hardly ever crossed again, although the Hamlyn Foundation, which he established, did contribute to a later venture with which I was connected.

In the early sixties my Chairman decided to set up a company to represent North American and British publishers in Europe. He chose the name Eurobooks at a time when many business companies were sticking Euro at the front of their activity, if it had any continental aspirations. Unfortunately, in our case, someone had beaten us to it and had already registered a British company with that name. Undismayed, the

Chairman, who had a property on the island of Sark in the Channel Islands registered it there and we became Eurobooks Limited of which I was the Executive Director, with the brief to establish its presence in every bookshop in Europe that sold English-language books. As there was only me and a secretary, that meant that I had to travel the length and breadth of Europe – from Moscow to Cork and from Tromsoe to Tenerife – in order to do this. This activity is known as representation and it is an interesting and exacting occupation.

I soon came to the conclusion that to be a successful and satisfied representative one had to be an introvert with oneself and an extrovert with others. This, because it entailed long periods alone travelling between cities and staying in hotels and so one had to be reasonably happy with one's own company. But then, when visiting the bookseller or his buyer there was a sudden switch, to relating to another person and enthusiastically presenting one's wares.

By good fortune or genetic inheritance I was gifted with this double faculty and I would recommend to anyone thinking of being a sales rep, or to any employer or personnel manager appointing them, that this characteristic should be present.

Most of the time I travelled in a company Dormobile, because I could load a lot of the books I was selling into it. I only once slept in the vehicle, and it was enough to put me off doing so again. I was rather too large to move around comfortably in what were then low-ceilinged vehicles. On that one time I had parked conveniently close to where I had business the next day. However, within minutes, police appeared telling me to move on and that, in no circumstances, could I leave it or live in it overnight. The place where I was obliged to go was miles away from my morning appointment.

For me the whole experience was a remarkable education in geography and people. I crossed the North Sea to Bergen and put my car on a train to Oslo, where I could collect it later. Bergen is Norway's second city and rich in history. I was able to visit the home of Edvard Grieg, the composer, and the theatre where Henrik Ibsen, the playwright, was a director. Not that I am a culture vulture, but when I had an hour or two between business calls, which I tried to average at four a day, I would visit places of interest. I would try to visit the art gallery of the towns that I went to. I enjoy art that portrays people doing things and regret that little of today's painting does that.

From Bergen I took a flight to Trondheim, a major fishing port and the home of Atlantic fish cooking. There is one very tasty item of herrings, which have been marinated in generous quantities of cognac or some hard liquor and left in barrels for a year or more. The combination of natural rotting and alcohol antisepsis produces a dish of exceptional savour that I first ate there.

Then on, by a further aerial hop, to Tromsoe, north of the Arctic Circle, home of a cathedral and the world's most northerly university, the latter being the main reason for my visit. The great stained glass window in Tromsoe Cathedral is hypnotic and glorious. I later met the artist who created it, Victor Sparre, who was a great friend of several Russian dissidents and was influential in Andrei Sakharov being awarded the Nobel Peace Prize.

I had come to believe that jealousies and conflicts between businessmen were of a pretty high order, but I discovered that they were easily topped by academics. I had to meet two professors in Bergen with different subjects in the same department. I had hoped to meet them together, but their secretary told me that this would not be possible, as they were not on speaking terms. It turned out that all communication between them was by way of messages through this secretary, without whose intervention the work of the department would not have been possible. I was told that they had a deep scientific difference of opinion, but surely there was also an emotive reason, perhaps such as different wartime allegiances or one making a pass at the other's wife.

Back to Bergen, where I took the night train through the mountains to Oslo. I missed some spectacular scenery, but you can't have everything. The first thing in Oslo was to find my car, which was located in a siding. It had been transported on an open wagon that was the first after the steam driven engine. Thus, subjected to soot and suffering the pollution of innumerable tunnels, the car's colour was transformed from light sea blue to funereal black. It had to be steam hand-washed at a garage, which took hours.

I liked Oslo. For a capital city it had more the feel of a very pleasant, but rather stark, country town. Within an hour I could walk to all my appointments at the bookshops and the university. I enjoyed being taken for a meal at Bloms Restaurant, made famous as the favourite eating place of generations of artists, whose, often self-created, coats-of-arms adorned the walls alongside paintings which had been accepted in lieu of payment for meals by hard-up painters of the day, one of whom was Picasso. A celebrated dish was 'black pot', the colour of the container, though happily not of the contents. The dish was nourishing and I can imagine it enabling poor artists to keep body and soul together for a low outlay.

Here I was tempted to do some conventional sightseeing and visited the Kontiki vessel in which Thor Heyerdal crossed the Pacific, and Roald Amundsen's ship which he took through the North-West Passage of Canada to the ocean beyond. But painting, as usual, had the better of it and I spent some hours in the gallery housing many of Edvard Munch's stunning works. But for visual art Gustav Vigeland's sculptures in Frogner Park are hard to beat. I particularly liked the one of a small boy in a temper waving his arms and stamping his feet, perhaps because I sometimes felt like that myself. In certain crisis situations I have often wondered if this was the only thing left to do. We would all feel better for it: compulsory jumping on the spot for frustrated politicians!

I learnt something about Nordic priorities when one First of

May I went to Turku Airport in Finland to catch a booked and ticketed flight to Stockholm. The airport seemed to be deserted, which I thought was rather odd. Then, when I came to the departure entrance the only sign of life was a rather dishevelled character with an airport cap. 'Why have you come?' he asked me, 'Don't you know that nothing moves on May Day.' 'But I have a ticket for a flight,' I said. 'Maybe, but you won't get out of here today. Come back tomorrow and they'll find you a place.' Quite unbelievingly I returned to my hotel, booked in again and wrote up my reports as my contribution to the celebration of the workers' struggle and the coming of spring.

I know that I should never lose my temper, that it is bad for me, that it shortens my life, that it upsets those around me or makes them laugh and, from whatever causes, it is usually my fault. However, sometimes emotion triumphs over logic and I explode. One such occasion was when I arrived in Athens late at night having driven all day from Belgrade, and found the room that I had booked had been given away. I came out of the hotel in a state of high dudgeon and took a hard kick at the first object I saw, which, unfortunately was made of concrete and dislocated my big toe. I managed to drive my car and find some fourth-rate lodgings with paper-thin walls where I soaked my aching foot in tepid water, listening to the couple in the room on one side having a lengthy, noisy quarrel and the couple on the other side making love. I was still seething but it didn't do me any good and I spent the next few days limping around Athens visiting reluctant booksellers. Since then it has been very hard to get me to fly off the handle, so it seems that a good lesson was learnt.

From Athens I drove to Istanbul via Salonica and the European Turkish coast. It was the first time that I had seen cultivated fields sweeping right down to the Mediterranean Sea, instead of villas, blocks of flats and highways. I imagine that this is no longer the case and that commercial development has spoiled the view. At Istanbul I had the pleasure of staying at the famous Pera Palas Hotel, but I sold no books.

I went to Russia at the time of Khruschev, when some minor reforms were beginning but, nevertheless, I had to move around within a prescribed framework. No sooner had I left the plane at Moscow's International Airport, than I heard my name over the loudspeakers asking me to come to a particular point. Having found it I was greeted by an airport official and asked to wait until a Dutch publisher, whom I had never met before, nor heard of, also arrived. He soon turned up and from then on we were treated as one, taken in the same chauffeur-driven saloon car from the airport, checked into the same hotel, given the same cultural programme (the Bolshoi, the Theatre of the Palace of the People, the Moscow Circus and the Science Park, where the original Sputnik was on display). We were allowed a different schedule of business visits and some variations on eating places, but that was all.

My negotiations with Mezhdunarodnaya Kniga, the Russian Export-Import Book Organisation, were curious, because the official dealing with me spoke English and the Head of the Department spoke French. As I did not speak Russian, all negotiations took place with me translating them between French and English. At least this showed that no one was vetting the exchange, unless it was being recorded and checked later. Somehow I don't think so. A system that checked every negotiation with every foreigner visiting Russia would be so voluminous as to be unworkable. Rather like the impossibility of a newspaper baron checking every word of all of his publications every day.

At Moscow University Library I had an unexpected and uncontrived meeting with two black students. They were furious about something and it turned out that one of them was being returned to his own country in Africa because he had begun dating a Russian girl. It seemed that the theoretical universalism of Communism did not extend to racial mixing between men and women. Apparently white students had protested to the authorities about this 'politically unaccept-able' relationship, and had demanded the African's expulsion from the country.

I was impressed by the mechanisation of book lending in the National Library. You found the cards of the books that you wanted, checked them into a machine and then waited for the books to arrive on a conveyor belt without any human intervention in the process. This was in the early Sixties, long before electronic wizardry had become known, let alone commonplace. I always suspected that this was a demonstra-tion model for foreign visitors, rather than general practice.

In Red Square I joined the queue to visit Lenin's embalmed body. One of the soldiers on duty must have been so concerned at seeing a well-dressed person and perhaps therefore, some-one in authority, waiting in a queue that he came to me and took me to the head of it and passed me inside the mausoleum. I was more impressed by that action than I was by the fixed-eyed corpse. And yet it disturbed me. Why had no one waiting in the queue protested? Was there a built-in acceptance of authority, when in a uniform or a good suit? I experienced it again 30 years later, well after the downfall of Communism, when a Russian friend took me to the head of a very long queue in a main-line station to buy a ticket, without a murmur from those patiently waiting. The people at the head of the queue even politely stood aside to let me in. We in Western Europe are not so acquiescent.

I am reminded of the wartime story, when queuing was widespread for scarce commodities, of the queue that formed outside a shop closed for lunch. A man went to the head of the queue and was manhandled to the back. He went up to the front again and was once more forced to the rear. Undaunted he tried for a third time and was grabbed again. 'All right,' he said, 'then I won't open the shop'. I must admit to having no patience with queue jumpers to this day, even old ladies, as I am often older than they are. However, in the Russian case, I fear that this easy acceptance of even minor injustices is a bad consequence of living for years under an oppressive system.

One day I hunted for a bookshop in a town in the south of France and eventually found it in a back street. I doubt if it sold a book in English in a season, but decided to try anyway. The owner was a nice man for he eventually ordered one copy of one title saying, 'C'est pour marquer votre passage.' ('It is a sign that you called by'). Perhaps the book is still there hidden away on one of his back shelves, several decades later.

The first time that I took the night ferry from Stockholm to Helsinki was before drive-on, drive-off existed and I held my breath as my car was wafted aboard on a rather delicate-looking sling. A great compensation on that ferry was the magnificent smorgasbord supper laid out on a 20-metre long buffet. The plates were rather small, but I became adept at constructing a Mount Everest of good things on a small base. Who but the Scandinavians can produce so many fine and tasty versions of the common herring?

I liked the simplicity of Helsinki with its wide streets and sturdy buildings. Sometimes I would go out to a nearby island park with examples of old-style Finnish houses and forest paths. The squirrels were so tame that they would climb up my trouser leg and fish into my jacket pockets to see if I was hiding anything edible. I usually came prepared and they were not disappointed.

Helsinki had two of the best bookshops in Europe and their sales of English-language books were phenomenal. The chief buyer of one of them, at the time that I was visiting, was a refugee Count from one of the Baltic States. When the Russians occupied his country he had somehow escaped across the often rough Baltic Sea in a small boat and found sanctuary in Finland. He still retained his polite and aristocratic manner and he was a good bookman into the bargain. I wonder if he lived to see his country free.

As our company was registered on the island of Sark, I had been able to open a bank account there. By local law every company had to have at least one Sark resident director and with us it was the bank manager. It turned out that his major activity was to be a director of companies and I would not have been surprised if he merited an item in the Guinness Book of Records as the person with the most company directorships. There were few taxes on the island, the main one being a small percentage of the value on buying a property. Alcoholic drinks were remarkably cheap which I don't suppose did much good to residents' livers.

I have a vivid recollection of being called back to London urgently on a very stormy day with great waves lashing around the coast and the regular boat service to Guernsey and the airport cancelled. Someone told me that he was going back in his motorboat and could give me a place. I still shudder when I think of the journey across several miles of raging sea, although strangely enough a small boat skimming the waves seems smoother than a larger one buffeting through them. So far I have never been sick at sea, although sometimes I am reduced to silence and morbid contemplation.

So much for a sales rep's life. In all I must have been close to the target of visiting every major bookshop in Europe and meeting the librarians of all the universities of the time. They were a nice lot of people and taught me more about the business of books than I could have ever learned sitting at a desk.

Sadly, John Grant and I parted on unhappy terms, which I think were largely based on misunderstandings. I had raised doubts about the veracity of our accounts and he suspected me of planning to join our largest client and of taking with me some of our other clients. Actually I had no such intention, but he was convinced that I did and gave me notice at home without the possibility of returning to the office to clear my desk. I suppose the explanation for this was that the only know-how and client information I could take with me was in my head and not on paper.

Once again I was without a job, but this time with a wife and son, a mortgage and no company car. Although I was now nearing 50, I was not so frantic as I had been ten years earlier, when I was sending off job applications at about two a day and wondering how much longer I would be able to eat. But at this time, lo and behold, an old friend told a Dutch multinational group, who wanted to develop into the United Kingdom, that I was available and the right man for them. After a meeting with two of their directors at Holland's Schiphol Airport and another one at their Head Office in Deventer, I got the job. I was taken on for a short term, two-year contract, to see how I performed. The Dutch are very careful. They even had a private detective check up on my business and personal reputation. Apparently the principal plus points were that I always paid my bills and had not been in prison. Thus began a relationship with the Dutch group Kluwer and later Wolters Kluwer, that was the most rewarding, professionally and financially, of my business life.

Working for a Multinational

I started with a secretary and one room, building up a new publishing venture located in the West London suburb of Brentford. We grew to a group of six companies with some 14 imprints, reaching out to most of the professional and many academic areas of national and world markets in less than a decade.

I profited from the visits and know-how of a managing director from the multinational group. He was Wouter (Walter) van Zeytveld and we became and still are good friends. Through many years Walter was a wise counsellor, rarely critical and always helpful. Although he was an Amsterdammer and a devoted supporter of the Ajax football club, his home was in a large village outside Deventer, in East Holland towards the German frontier. Deventer was named after a monk of the Middle Ages, called Daventrius, who must have got around at the time, because he also founded Daventry in England.

By the end of my decision-making career I felt that there was a strong case for charging more for a short book than a longer one. This, of course, came up against the conventional pricing policy that you could charge according to the number of pages. This often led to the abuses of padding out the text and raising the type size. However, if the author and the publisher work together to produce the shortest possible text consistent with clarity and completeness, that enables the busy person to get the information needed without waste of time. In my view that would justify as high a price as one might charge for a book twice as long, taking twice the time to read, for the same gain of information and instruction. If time is money, this is a justifiable way of saving it.

I am reminded of the case where I had sold the American rights for a book that would be printed in the UK. I received a message from the New York publisher asking me how much the book weighed. I asked him what that had to do with the deal. He wrote back saying that he priced his books according to weight and therefore I should use the heaviest possible paper in the manufacture of his edition. If you visit a bookshop in the USA you will find that new hardbound books are bigger than their European counterparts and this must have something to do with the weight plus size argument for a stiff price.

I once had an enlightened chairman who told me to turn the management structure plan on its head, putting him at the bottom and the customers on the top line. In Kluwer I had a group director whose companies were earning half the profits of the entire multinational, who always took a train or bus from the airport and never a cab, wore a plain mac instead of a fur-lapelled overcoat, and asked us to work out of unpretentious premises.

Nevertheless, I do think that appearances matter, in dress and manners and in the style of buildings and of office interiors. No one works well in dowdy surroundings nor when managed by scruffy people and when using uncared-for or outdated equipment. The right balance in all things may seem old-fashioned but it is the best policy.

When you are publishing books or magazines or newspapers or putting information on line you are doing it for readers who are much more than customers. They are citizens of our human society and unless you are reacting to their needs, hopes, fears, aspirations and levels of intelligence you should be in another job. I always felt that my most essential task as a publisher was to establish friendly and helpful relationships with my authors. They were a priority for my office time and my social life. I remember one author, who had written books for several firms, saying that working with us was like driving a Rolls Royce as compared with an old banger. I went home feeling very happy that night.

This care for authors may and probably should involve care for their family life. I would always try to meet their wives, if they were married, and my wife was always endeavouring to persuade single men to tread the path of matrimony. There was a time when we were trying to persuade three exceptionally talented and busy professionals to edit a book for us. They wanted to do it, because they felt that it would be helpful to their fellows and improve standards of performance, but their wives did not see enough of them as it was.

We hit on the idea of inviting them and their wives to spend a weekend at a pleasant country hotel in a Dutch beauty spot, including an evening in Amsterdam. The wives took part in all our planning sessions, so that they would understand the project and see how useful it would be to less experienced practitioners. They became enthusiastic partners and one even told her husband that he should skip Saturday morning golf for a year in order to do the book.

Those three men became one of the happiest and most productive teams that we ever worked with and became friends for life with one another and with the publishers. The book was a great success and had more reviews in its subject than any other publication in the field. One reader rang me up to say that the book had done more for his profession at a stroke than years of training schemes.

Many people think that publishers sit in their offices waiting for writers or agents to send in manuscripts and then decide whether to publish them or not. This may be partly true for fiction publishers, who hope that at least one in a 100 budding writers will produce a best seller. It is the big sellers that make the real money and recoup the losses on less successful titles.

But this is not true for professional and academic books. In a ten-year span of this type of publishing, I can only recall two cases of publishing an unsolicited manuscript. What happened in most cases was that we would spend time in studying a particular subject area and in meeting people who were involved with it, looking for important gaps in the supply of information and expertise. Having identified a gap and feeling that it had enough content to justify a book, I would make a market test to find out if a cross section of the potential buyers agreed that a book on that subject would be helpful to them. I called this a concept test. That is different from a product test such as can be done with a new type of chocolate bar, when you try the bar out on say a 1000 people and if enough of them like it, multiplied by the size of the customer market to justify the risk, you go ahead and manufacture, backed up by a powerful advertising campaign.

It is pretty obvious that one cannot produce a thousand copies of a book to try out on the market, as the costs would be prohibitive. So a concept test is the best way to back up research and to be in a position to take a reasonable risk. There are still some 'hunch' publishers who hope that there will be enough 'impulse' buyers to cover their outlay. I never felt confident enough to join that optimistic group.

If you are reasonably independent and can be profitable with bread-and-butter lines, you may be able to dabble in your own special interest subjects. I know a very successful medical publisher, whose real interest was classical music, and brought out a line in musicology whose titles rarely sold more than a few hundred copies but provided great satisfaction to fellow enthusiasts.

I still keep on my shelves a title whose obscurity fascinates me. It is called *The Logic of Invariable Concomitance in the Tattvacintamani*. Out of kindness to the publisher whom I knew well, I hesitate to name the low figure of people who might possibly need this book, let alone buy it. But that is what libraries are for, to enable people to read books that they could not afford to buy, particularly scholars and paupers.

Sometimes I was bewildered by booksellers' methods of selection. There was a case of one who would sniff a copy of the book before deciding. Not that many of them can get the chance to do that, as they would be buying sight unseen from catalogues, book jackets and reviews. It so happened that in my early days I carried a few copies with me and I saw this buyer smell each of them in turn and place them into two piles, one for those that he would order and the other for his rejections. There was another, I think at a university on Tenerife, one of the Canary Islands, who was much more devoted to advising me as to the best restaurants and bathing beaches in the locality than in ordering any of my wares. I took his advice and stayed on for a week at one of the resorts!

For me a major compensation for hard work with authors was the entry which they gave me into many sectors of national life – to Parliament, to the great industrial companies, to the City of London, to the big banks, to the world of medicine with its surgeons, hospitals and research bodies, to the Bar and the Solicitors' Law Society, to top law practices and world-renowned accounting firms, to the Farmers' Union, the Horticultural Society, to major builders, estate agents and even to kidnap consultants. There was hardly a corner of the way the world worked that I did not have access to.

Our task, through our authors and subject editors, was to provide information and expertise to the professionals in as many sectors as possible. In choosing writers I was looking for authority and lucidity. Firstly, they had to know what they were writing about and, equally important, to express it in an understandable way. The second quality is more rare than one might expect. Not all good teachers are effective writers. And not all eggheads can explain what they know to others. An enemy of clarity is jargon and I reproduce a few lines from an Instant Jargon Generator, a table in which any arrangement of the words between the three columns produces a plausible but meaningless expression:

1	2	3
Curricular	Research	Project
Behavioural	Simulation	Validation
Programmed	Implementation	Assessment
Cognitive	Examination	Objectives
Instructional	Participation	Resources

One disquieting experience was to discover that a misprinted word in an author's introduction became a jargon expression! As most of our publications were major works in themselves, we usually heralded their arrival with a launch party, at some appropriate venue such as the Institute of Directors Pall Mall Centre, the Stationers Hall, the Law Society Library, New Zealand House or a suitable top hotel. Sometimes they took the form of a lunch but, more usually, an early evening reception. The British custom is to offer drinks and snacks on arrival and finish up with laudatory speeches. The theory is that the guests will not listen until softened up with alcohol and food. Strangely, continentals take the opposite view, with speeches first and goodies as a reward for attentive listening at the end. Take your pick.

My favourite location was at one of the atmosphere-filled rooms in the Houses of Parliament, kindly arranged by a friendly Member or Lord. Some of our guests would take the opportunity to buy a bottle of Houses of Parliament-labelled sherry, whether for the quality of the drink or the one-upmanship of the label, I was never quite sure.

The Institute of Directors now uses the splendid building that once housed the United Services Club and the deal included the paintings of successful soldiers and battles won. I once mischievously made the suggestion that the paintings of admirals, generals and marshals of the Air Force might be replaced by portraits of big business men. However it was felt that the glamour of splendid uniforms and decorations would not be bettered by pin-striped suits and dinner jackets. At one of our occasions we had a senior American guest, who when I showed him the truly magnificent main staircase with vast paintings of the battles of Waterloo and Trafalgar at either side, remarked, 'Gee Bill, that unused space must be worth at least a million dollars.'

During our early years we had a partnership with the Harrap Company. Its Chairman, Paull Harrap, and I became friends. He would sometimes entertain me at the Wig and Pen Club, which was in one of the few buildings that survived the Great Fire of London in 1666. It was a warren of small rooms and twisting staircases, but the food was well cooked and the staff good-tempered. And what could beat the cachet of dining in rooms more than 300 years old? At one period my son Fred was training to cook in the Club kitchens and he would come up from below to shake hands. He certainly learned how to prepare a good steak there.

Paull told me that he had been born in Australia and brought up in Ireland. When I asked him what nationality that made him, he said, 'Even when a horse is born in a cowshed, it is still a horse.' The Irish period gave him a love of horse racing and he would get away to the Ascot and Epsom tracks whenever he could. He was a great supporter of innovation and enjoyed our working together in fields of publishing that were new to him. And I learned a lot from him about senior management practice that stood me in good stead later.

After a couple of years in cramped offices we moved into a new building in the old town centre, overlooking the River Brent and a canal wharf. Amazingly enough, a pair of king-fishers had established themselves in the vicinity and I often glimpsed the rainbow colours of those birds as they hunted for fish and fed their chicks. It was here that we made the change-over from mechanical addressing and accounting systems to

modern electronics in the shape of a Nixdorf computer instal-
lation. We had been told that the new equipment would be up
and running within two or three weeks. What nobody had
seen fit to tell us was that it would take some months of
manual work to transfer our old addressograph mailing lists of
more than 100,000 names and addresses onto the computer
base. So having moved the old machines into our parking area,
we were obliged to resuscitate them with no climatic protection for our operators.

Our third move was to refurbished premises to our design
on the Great West Road, where major firms were situated. We
were sandwiched, if that is the right expression, between
Gillette of razorblade renown and Firestone of car tyre fame.
I got to know the heads of both companies. Eventually Firestone decided to close down their plant and the site was rede-
veloped. The Firestone building had a rather flamboyant, art
deco style front. It was threatened with a preservation order,
and to have had to maintain it would have been a serious
problem for the developers. The order was due to come into
force on the Monday following the week in which it was
served. Wasting no time, the new owners called in a major site-
clearance firm who dismantled the front wall in question
during the weekend, so that it was no longer in existence when
the order came into effect. That's one way of dealing with a
problem! I was rather glad at the time, because I had never
liked the style, which I had described as being Mussolini
Fascist.

Brooks Firestone told me that the company made more
money from the sale of the factory freehold than they did from
making tyres during the entire time that they were in the UK.
He did not stay with the family firm, but used his share of the
fortune to buy vineyards in California and to make 'Firestone'
wine. I was later able to buy some in my local wine store and
it was pretty good. Brooks made a British conquest by marry-
ing the daughter of the Bishop of Guildford.

1. My mother

2. Dad on his 70th birthday

3. With my sister, Mariane Willett

4. Staff at 17 Indian Infantry Brigade HQ, December 1945. I am third from left, standing.

5. With the Eighth
Army in Italy during
World War II

6. Winston Churchill addressing the Council of Europe, 1949.
I am centre back row on the press benches.

7. In Mukundgarh, Rajasthan desert, 1957,
Mataden Bagheria at the helm

8. Maurice Mercier, General Secretary,
French Textile Workers Union

9. Myself and Sonja (on right) at the annual dinner of the British Institute of Directors, 1976

10. British Day,
Le Touquet,
October 1991

11. Introducing Prince
Edward to British
Association members in
northern France,
August 1995

My link with the Chairman of Gillette came when he headed up a committee to raise money for building an Arts Centre on the Thamesside. My firm was not able to contribute much money; but we did make our offices available for committee meetings and to help with publicity. Together with grants from the municipality we succeeded, and the Watermans Arts Centre was constructed and has since served the cultural needs of the community. I believe that it was one of the first arts centres, after World War II, to be created by private initiative.

I was a Vice-President of the Brentford Chamber of Commerce. We received a strong complaint from citizens living in the streets surrounding Brentford's First Division Football Club. They were concerned about the vast quantities of rubbish and beer cans left for several hundred yards around the stadium after the Saturday afternoon match, which were not cleared by the municipality until the Wednesday of the following week. They asked the Chamber to intervene and get something done about it. We also complained to the Council, but were told that the schedule was fixed and could not be changed for the convenience of those lucky enough to live close to the football ground.

Then we had the idea to meet with the leaders of the complaint and to suggest that they form voluntary street teams who would clear the streets after each game. We, the Chamber, would provide skips for them to put the rubbish into and these would be emptied by the Council on their Wednesday routine visit. This was agreed to and the result was that the streets were cleaned up within two hours of the end of a match. It provided a good example of citizens' initiative, which later I was able to describe to friends in Russia, who were also complaining about municipal shortcomings. Having lived in a vertically controlled society, the idea of lateral initiatives was foreign to them. Both in Moscow and in Nizhny Novgorod, the great city on the Volga, I had noticed that people kept their own apartments in good order, but the public areas were in decay and no one cut the grass surrounding the buildings. The Brentford example gave them the idea to set up teams to deal with some of their own problems.

I was amused by a new finance director, who had not previously worked in the publishing business, when he asked me, 'Why do you publish some titles that lose money?' The answer is that we don't do it deliberately. We intended that every book we published would make money and in some cases a lot. It was also our intention to publish works that would help the buyers to do their job better in professional and academic fields. When we would risk a first-book loss it was with the intention of establishing a lead in the subject area or to gain a potentially valuable author. Such books could be described as 'loss-leaders'.

I had a sense of human relations and the importance of sound personnel policies. And this approach was strongly supported by the holding company. One day I tried to reassure the personnel chief of the holding group that my door was always open to any of the staff who wanted to talk to me with complaints, problems or suggestions. 'Yes', he said, 'but your door has a very high step.' I assumed from this that there was something in my attitude that made employees think twice before coming to see me. What could it be? Did they think that I would be too clever for them? That I would only represent company policy and not have an independent assessment? That it could somehow be a black mark against them for pay and promotion? I was never really sure as to the reason and the personnel chief did not enlighten me but, nevertheless, I did try to make it known that I was always happy to meet anyone in an open-minded spirit.

As we rise in the business hierarchy we learn and are taught a lot about managing downwards and even sideways with our peers, but the subject of managing upwards is not touched upon. I suppose that, if you are on top, you don't want anyone below trying to influence your style or your actions. But to me it seemed important, particularly as in a subsidiary company you were reporting to more senior people. I recalled a case when my Chairman at the time always made at least one alteration to any written proposal that we made to him. In view of this I would make some obvious mistake or unlikely recommendation, which had nothing to do with my real proposition. The result was that he easily spotted these errors, corrected them and returned the basic proposal unaltered.

The happy outcome of my time with Kluwer Publishing Limited was that we were successfully publishing professional books and journals and had begun to develop electronic publishing with medical databases. We soon passed the million pound turnover mark and, best of all, were providing employment to more than 50 people.

Reaching for the Top

In 1984 I handed over Kluwer Publishing Limited to my successor, Colin Ancliffe, and moved to offices in central London as Deputy Chairman of Kluwer UK. My main tasks now were to develop our law and insurance publishing, to handle our acquisition policy and to represent Kluwer in trade associations and to the public.

We were situated in Kingsway, a broad street with the Law Courts and Fleet Street on the east side and Covent Garden and the Strand on the other. At its southern end was Bush House, where the BBC World Service dwelt, with the Thames closely beyond. Our main theatres were within easy reach and it was only a short walk to the HQ of the Publishers Association. All in all an ideal location for what I had to do. During the following years I was Chairman of the Publishers Law Panel, on the National Committee of the Periodical Publishers Association and Chairman of its Luncheon Club, and Deputy Chairman of Publishers Databases Ltd, a company set up to encourage and develop electronic publishing at its outset. I had a finger in many pies and I enjoyed the ubiquity and challenge of the role. I held all these positions until I finally retired three years after the normal date of 65. For many years after retirement I was a consultant to publishing firms in London and Paris.

On the Law Panel, possibly the toughest issue that we had to deal with was the Association's official attitude towards the appearance of Salman Rushdie's *The Satanic Verses*. The parent publishing company was the monumental firm of Longmans and it turned out that the book was published without the advance knowledge of senior directors, not unusual in the case of another book from an established author. Nevertheless, in view of the uproar that the book caused, it was rather surprising that no-one in the publishing chain had voiced any qualms. It turned out later that some had, but they had not reached the ears of the top executives.

On the Committee we were concerned, but not so much as we would have been today, about the negative effect of the book on Muslims in Britain and across the world. In the end we expressed the view that Longmans and other firms should be more careful in the future, but that, in the interests of freedom of expression and freedom to publish, we supported its appearance.

Some years later, when in India, I discovered that Longmans' senior executive in New Delhi had refused to publish the book in India on the grounds that it could foment communal dissent and violence. I could not imagine how this had not registered with some senior person back in London. I learned that one of Britain's best-known imams had been shown a copy of the manuscript before publication and asked to comment on it. He told them that whilst he did not agree with the implications of the book that, if certain pages – which turned out to be the most offending ones – were expressed in more moderate language, he would not oppose it. No attention was paid to this advice and unchanged publication went ahead with the results that we know.

It was praiseworthy of the British Government that they decided to protect Rushdie against death threats and safeguarded him in secure locations for many years, no doubt at some cost to the State purse. That the threats were not hollow was shown by the assassination of the Japanese translator and the shooting of the Norwegian publisher in front of his own house. He fortunately survived the attack. One leading French publisher told me that his firm had sold 290,000 copies of the

French edition, but lost money on it because of the security precautions they had to put in place for their own staff and for some booksellers.

Came the day when the Data Protection Act was passed by Parliament. The intention was to protect the privacy of the individual against the public availability of any medical, financial, personal or embarrassing information about him. Every person would have the right to see what information was held about him or her and to have inaccurate or offending material removed.

I decided to hold several meetings of publishers and their staff to have the law explained to them by one of our legal advisers and to raise questions and be given answers. One view expressed was that this was a law to protect people with something to hide and would be a damn nuisance to everybody else; that the average law-abiding citizen does not worry about what others know about him. Whilst I had some sympathy with this opinion, I had to insist that we were now dealing with the law of the land and that it had to be obeyed. Those of us with electronically stored information about our staff, our authors and our customers would have to register our databases with the Data Protection Authority, and make sure that the information was not inaccurate or defamatory.

Panic stations ensued in our companies, particularly with the in-house editors who stored information about their authors, sometimes of a very frank nature, such as: 'He is totally unreliable.' 'John X is frequently drunk.' 'He made passes at me,' and so on. Rapid efforts were made to erase any such offending material. In practice very few people ever asked for access and if they did, I suspect that it was to make sure that any financial information corresponded to that given on their tax returns.

Being on the Council of the Periodical Publishers Association (PPA) was an enjoyable experience. Its Chief Executive was a Conservative Member of Parliament, Tim Hoosen, and its Director was Michael Finley who had been Britain's youngest daily newspaper editor. Michael and I became good friends and he later joined me in working with the International Communications Forum and for some years administer its funding appeals. My work with the PPA probably brought myself and Sonja invitations to the Queen's Garden Party at Buckingham Palace on two occasions. As we lived close at hand in Knightsbridge it was an easy walk to get there and it was pleasing to be rubbing shoulders with the 'good and great' of the land. Apart from the frisson of seeing the Queen and members of the Royal Family close at hand, the tea and refreshments, especially the ice cream, were 'worth the detour' as the Michelin guide says.

For some reason at meetings of the PPA Council we were not allowed to discuss salary and personnel matters. An off-the-record luncheon club was established of which I eventually became the Chairman. It was here that we got the inside story of what was going on in wage negotiations by the big magazine groups, how claims for paid maternity leave by male staff were being dealt with and how things were going at employment tribunals. This had little to do with the content of our periodicals, but it was the nitty-gritty of the management side of our lives.

In the early Eighties the electronic outreach into publishing was but a small cloud on the horizon. But on a business trip to the USA I realised that non-publishing companies, particularly computer hardware and software firms, were trying to get in on the act, particularly in the area of electronic databases. I voiced my concern that, unless we took action, we would be beaten to the gate in this field.

Clive Bradley, Chief Executive at the Publishers Association, had been thinking in the same way and our efforts led to the setting up of Publishers Databases Ltd with the purpose of encouraging publishers to enter the field and, possibly, to set up some databases ourselves. Our Chairman was Sir Harry

Hookway, Head of the British Library and a forward-looking personality, and I became the Deputy Chairman. Our practical achievements were not very great, but we did beat the drum on the subject and some of our major publishers, particularly Butterworths in the legal field, set about pioneering work.

My own company set an example by preparing a drug treatment database of which a special feature was to indicate any dangers of prescribing two or more drugs at the same time when there might be dangerous side effects. In the UK doctors had the right to prescribe about 4,000 pharmaceutical products, which number would give the possibility of some 15 million interactions between two drugs. This was manifestly something that could not be dealt with in print, and we began to set up a database, so that when a doctor tapped in the names of any two drugs he planned to prescribe, it would come up with the answer on screen in seconds, as to whether they were safe together, should not be given to pregnant patients, or would cause a rash, or even death.

You would have thought that doctors, particularly GPs, would have leapt at such a service. But this was in the days before most people used a computer or carried a mobile phone. There was resistance to installing another telephone line and to the subscription charge. Saving a few deaths would not justify the cost and effort. There was an equal resistance in law firms to accepting the new technology, which may come as a surprise to those who are born tapping a keyboard and could not imagine a world without screens.

One of the most enlightening aspects of my work was that of finding and negotiating acquisitions of companies that would strengthen our own base, increase our turnover and hopefully add to our profitability. Why are companies ready to be bought? I suppose the main reasons are that the owners or shareholders would rather have the money than the hassle and risk; that a sole owner has no willing heirs and wants to retire; that the owners fear that the company will not weather the financial and marketing storms ahead; or that they receive an offer which they can't refuse.

We had just acquired a company when I received a phone call from one of their authors in Canada, saying that he was coming to London and would like to have breakfast with me at The Athenaeum, an exclusive club in London, whose members were mainly top civil servants, bishops and scientists. He warned me in advance that his book, published by this company, had been very badly handled, had cost him expected but unrealised royalties, had adversely affected his academic status and had caused great stress to his wife. He estimated that the value of all this was in the neighbourhood of a million Canadian dollars and that he expected my firm, as the new publishers of the work, to compensate him for this amount. I did not feel that we could be held responsible for the shortcomings of the previous owners, if shortcomings they were. It is a natural tendency of authors to think that their books are not being properly marketed. I have had several cases of writers who pop into the most unlikely booksellers for their subject and are disappointed to find that their book is not in stock.

As a million Canadian dollars might be at stake, I consulted my colleagues in Holland. The upshot was that I was to hold firm and tell the man to go ahead and sue us in the courts, and that not a penny of compensation was to be given. One pleasure of the Athenaeum is that the breakfasts are very good, so I enjoyed it and listened him out.

By far the largest part of the million dollars was to be allocated for relief of his wife's stress, a lesser amount to recover his reputation and the remaining smaller sum for expected royalties. I then informed him that he could do his worst, but my firm was not going to fork out for a book which they did not commission and had had no part in its promotion and sales. Furthermore, we were not minded to negotiate a settlement. To give him his due he gasped and then laughed and said, 'Well, it was worth a try and I had to come to London anyway, but I shall not be submitting my next book for you to publish.' So, on a rather civilised note we went our ways.

Kluwer were the largest law publishers in continental Europe and it was certainly the major part of their profitability. But they had no toehold in England until my firm appeared on the scene. British law publishing was dominated by Butterworths and Sweet & Maxwell. Most of our professional handbooks dealt with aspects of the law affecting each particular activity, but when I moved to central London we had the temerity to start up a Kluwer Law imprint. We looked to acquire any small law publishing fish that were ready to be caught; they were few and far between. We did make friends with the veteran publisher, Barry Rose in the old Sussex town of Chichester, and were able to acquire his bound law titles to give us something of a start. We also appointed Elizabeth Bramwell, who had edited the *Law Gazette,* as our publisher and managing director of the imprint. I like to think that I might have been the first man to appoint a woman managing director in the book publishing arena but have not claimed an entry in the *Guinness Book of Records*!

This paddling on the edges of the law pool, plus my activities with the Publishers' Association, led me to meet and make friends with Gordon Graham, the Chairman and Chief Executive of the famous Butterworths, themselves to be bought up later by a rival multinational, Reed Elsevier. I think that we liked one another's style and our friendship lasted through to the setting up of the International Communications Forum, and it continues to this day.

The French Connection

In the early Seventies when my status and finances were in better condition, I responded to my friend Maurice Mercier's recommendation that it was a good idea to buy a property in France. He had retired himself by that time and was living close to Cahors, so we decided to look in South West France in the departments of the Dordogne and Lot and Garonne, especially the latter being considered as *la France profonde*, i.e. off the beaten track and out of touch with modern life.

We spent two weeks of our summer holiday visiting place after place, varying from broken down large sheds to mini châteaux. At one house there were no toilet arrangements at all and when we asked the property agent what was the procedure, he pointed to a shovel and said 'They take that out into the field'. We passed on that one.

Almost at the end of our stay we found an old place with walls a metre thick that turned out to have been a *dépendance du château*, probably a hunting lodge of the Château de Lauzun. It was structurally in good condition, although inside it had been curiously and wantonly abused by the previous occupants. They had luridly painted over the splendid stonework, packed ancient kitchen equipment into a lovely open fireplace and left everywhere in a right mess. This condition must have been putting off buyers because the asking price was very low.

Sonja and I felt that behind these horrors was an attractive building and we also liked the quiet hamlet in which it was situated and the long views across the rolling countryside. So we made an offer and it was accepted. The hamlet was called *Queysaguet* which we were told was old French for 'Who goes there?' and must have been on one of the front lines during the Hundred Years War between France and England in the Middle Ages.

Then began the work of restoration, which in the end cost as much as buying the place, but by and large we enjoyed it. For reasons of propriety, as it would otherwise have been impossible to invite friends to stay, the first priority was to construct the facilities to have a flush toilet and to block off the existing earth closet with its flat, wooden seat and a deep drop into the underground. This was quite a major work involving digging out a deep hole for a sewage tank some distance from the house and installing complete bathroom facilities. It was a day for celebration when all that was built and working.

It had been in my mind that this second home would become a place where I would think great publishing thoughts and conceive future best sellers and new journals. That never happened! There was something about the place that induced in me a sense of complete relaxation; the quiet countryside, the pollution-free atmosphere with clear sparkling night skies, watching the satellites fly over and the vast reaches of a really Milky Way, the singing of birds, the croaking of frogs and the rustle of rabbits scattering along the hedgerows. And within the house the comfort of metre-thick stone walls, the logs blazing in an open fireplace, the rain pattering softly on the sweeping tiled roofs, the smell of a roast cooking in the kitchen and the gentle knock on the door of a passing neighbour. In the early days there was no telephone, no television, very occasional letters, just as complete an isolation as one can experience in our bustling, frenetic Western world. It was for me an island of sanity in a mad society.

The area was becoming increasingly popular with British second-home seekers buying up old properties, usually empty farm houses resulting from more successful farmers taking over their neighbours' land at bargain prices, but having no use for the house and buildings. At that time I had no wish to fraternise with the local Brits, as I saw enough of them back in London. Sonja did not have the same hang-up as me and did strike up some friendships with fellow foreigners.

We were fortunate in being able to speak reasonable French and it always amazed me how many of my fellow Anglo-Saxons were prepared to buy second homes and sometimes even small businesses without being able to put a sentence together in the language. On the other hand I never met a French person, even lawyers and doctors, in Lot and Garonne who could speak English.

After about eight years we realised that the disadvantage of a second home is that you feel obliged to go there for every holiday and miss the variety of visiting other places. Also an old property, we were told that it was 600 years of age, takes a lot of looking after and uses up much money. There were always tiles blowing off the roof and other storm damage, the garden got overgrown during our absences and the drive down there seemed longer and longer.

In any event we had not considered it as a retirement house. It had been more of an adventure and an experience, and the satisfaction of restoration and landscaping had ended. So, not without sadness, we sold it for a reasonable sum and transferred our attentions to a house in Wiltshire, which was only two hours' drive from London.

Then, about one year before my retirement from active business, my wife said to me one evening, 'Why don't we find a house on the continent for when you retire? It is always such a fuss when we travel abroad, driving to a port, booking the tickets, going across the Channel, getting off the boat, then finding somewhere to stay for the first night in France.' I was swayed by her argument, although I suspected that she had become somewhat claustrophobic living on the British side of the English Channel. She would probably have been happier had the Channel Tunnel been opened and made train or car journeys much more simple. But that was after her death.

So one weekend we took a trip over to Le Touquet where we had often stayed, and had liked it with its wide, light sandy beaches, its villa-peppered forest and old style Anglo-Norman streets. With no great pretensions we bought a small apartment in a condominium close to the sea, just behind the dunes and a strip of pine trees.

When we first took the *Mer et Soleil* flat I still had a year to run in my work with Wolters Kluwer, but Sonja wanted to move over right away. 'Can't you commute?' she asked me. 'You can use our Cadogan Place flat during the week and be here for the weekends.' It looked like a tall order, but on investigation, I found that I could drive to the hovercraft port near Boulogne, cross the Channel in 40 minutes to Folkestone and then on to London in less than two hours, somewhere between three and four hours in all. I then agreed with my firm that I could commute on Monday morning and return on Friday afternoon, giving me three nine-hour days and two four-hour days, being a 35-hour week in all, which even as long ago as that was the company norm. So for a year I commuted in this way. Was I London's longest-distance commuter? I could not have been far off.

For a time I took a considerable interest in the British Association for Northern France and for some years was its Vice President for the departments of the Pas de Calais and the Somme. It was estimated that there were about 3,000 British residents in the five Northern departments, of whom one third had jobs, one third were retired and the other third married to French spouses (or 'spice'?). These figures did not include the many Brits who owned holiday flats and houses in the region, who must number several thousand more. A major feat was to organise with the Mayor, Léonce Deprez, a British Day at Le

Touquet to which 1,200 came, enjoyed a lunch given in the Hotel School and were shown the sights and the shops.

Perhaps I am an exemplary citizen or just one who hasn't been found out, but following several years as a French resident, but remaining a British citizen, I was asked by the Consul General for the five Northern Departments of France, located at Lille, the area's major city, to be a Consular official for the *sous-préfecture* in which I was located. The specific title is Consular Correspondent and this is surely the lowest form of unpaid diplomatic life. He was persuasive and I was pleased, if not honoured, to be asked and I accepted. As a matter of fact it did not turn out to be too exacting a task, particularly as Le Touquet and its surrounding area is rather well-behaved and has good municipal leadership.

What are the duties of a humble voluntary consular officer? The first is to help any British citizen in difficulty or to restrain him or her in the event of their incurring the wrath of the local citizenry. An example of the first was an Englishman and his family on their first journey to the continent for a holiday on the Mediterranean, who became victim to the priority-from-the-right regulation in French built-up areas. British driving reflexes are not prepared for this on a first visit and as a result I would estimate there are several hundred incidents per year in our Northern French towns.

In this case the car was not very substantial and due to the greater size of the French vehicle was damaged beyond easy repair. I met the Englishman in the middle of the road with broken car parts scattered around and a very distressed wife and two children. Their car was in a terminal state and their long looked-forward-to holiday gone. I helped the two drivers complete their compulsory accident insurance forms. At least the Brit would recover the present value of his car, probably not very much, and he would not be spending the night in a French gaol. But what to do with two weeks holiday time in hand? I managed to persuade him that Le Touquet was a very enjoyable and well-equipped holiday town and that I could find his family a reasonably priced local hotel.

The other side of the coin is when the French complain about the behaviour of my co-citizens. For example, when they will not pay their restaurant or hotel bills. On being phoned by the local owner, my policy has been to inform the police and to ask that a uniformed officer and I would arrive at the hotel or restaurant in question together in ten minutes time. This always works as, when confronted by dual authority, the culprits quickly discover that they do have a credit card or currency after all, and quietly pay up. After one settlement two scruffy young men asked the police to give them a ride to the railway station and were unceremoniously told what they could do with themselves.

The second task of the honorary consul is to establish friendly relations with the local mayors, parliamentarians and leading citizens. This I enjoyed doing, as it led to many friendships and to being frequently included in civic activities. This side of things includes making arrangements for official visits by the Consul General, diplomats and senior British people. I have lived through four Consul Generals as they are changed every so often.

I had to organise the local British presence for the Anglo-French Summit between Prime Minister Blair and President Chirac in February 2003, being held in Le Touquet, doubtless due to our Député Maire Deprez's support of the President in the National Parliament. Having assembled our local patriotic British at a fashionable bar, we moved together to a reserved front-of-the-crowd vantage point to welcome our leaders. They duly arrived and, having inspected the ceremonial guard, came straight across to our waving Union Jacks and chatted with us for a minute or two. Consequently, we were the first to be pictured by the TV cameras and news photographers and our faces went round the world. A friend rang me up the next day from Ireland saying that he had seen me on the TV news and, several weeks later friends in India told me the same story. Such is fleeting fame, fortuitously acquired in the shadow of the great! Next day I was pictured in the regional paper as 'the most Touquetois of the British'.

Quite recently I was presented with the Medaille d'Honneur en Or of Le Touquet by the mayor in the Town Hall, surrounded by many local friends. A very happy occasion.

II

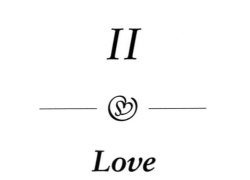

Love

My guide in Rijeka

Back in the days when I was trying to make a living as a free-lance journalist, I was staying in the beautiful resort town of Opatija, built during the time of the Austro-Hungarian Empire when that short stretch of the Adriatic was their one opening to the sea. Nearby was Yugoslavia's main port of Rijeka, formerly *Fiume* in Italian, both words meaning river. The actual river there was called the Rijeka Rijeka. I wanted to write an article about the town. But how to tackle the subject?

I asked the girl who handled travellers' cheques in the local travel office if she knew anyone who spoke English and who could show me around Rijeka. She said, 'Yes! I think that our legal adviser would be a good person.' It was agreed that she would arrange for us to meet for a coffee at ten o'clock the next morning. I arrived, expecting a man, and to my surprise found a devastatingly attractive woman called Sonja. She had red hair and I was always susceptible to that colour. She suggested that we visited Rijeka right away and led me to the bus stop. The single-decker bus had a sign saying, '12 seated and 84 standing', which seemed both an overlarge number and the wrong way round. I was more used to London double-deckers with six standing and 58 seated. But as we got closer to town, it became apparent why standing room had the priority. It was an area of many people and few buses. There was no end to people getting on, but getting off was harder.

Finally we made it after passing a great oil refinery and moving along the docks road. Every quay had a ship being loaded or unloaded, and out in Kvarner Bay were many more at anchor waiting their turn. My guide knew the whole scene from A to Z, was friendly with a number of the ships' captains and port administrators, and knew the fishermen who harvested the local waters. She was also in touch with theatre people, hotel owners and the restaurateurs. I could not have had a better guide.

I never wrote that article about Rijeka, as my priorities steadily shifted away from the pursuit of a story to the pursuit of the lady. For someone who had held out for a long time from getting too deeply committed to the opposite sex, my defences were rapidly crumbling. I lost interest in the statistics of the tonnage entering the port and the nature of imports and exports and the capacity of the oil refinery. The opinions of the civic, political and business leaders about the success of the town's activities began to pall. Anyway, most of them were repeating material churned out by backroom Communist functionaries. What I did enjoy was walking for hours with my guide along the old town streets and the sea front, drinking wine and eating scampi with her in numerous taverns and visiting the homes of her friends.

The latter included a retired ship's captain and his elegant wife. The captain delighted in telling stories of their wedding when he was so fearful of taking the step, that, even in the church, he hid behind a pillar and had to be manhandled by his two best men into an appropriate place beside the bride. Was this a portent of how I would feel myself before long?

I recall a restaurant on the top of the Neboder Hotel, *neboder* meaning skyscraper, about 20 storeys high, which made it easily the tallest building in the town. The view across the city and the bay to the distant islands was breathtaking. Sonja talked about her past and so I began to learn about her amazing life and the fantastic resilience of her character.

I realise that I may want to avoid or gloss over some parts of the story and other parts I may want to heighten or exaggerate. Even so I shall try to express the message of her life and hope so that the truth will shine through – her experiences, her day-to-day ways of living, her explorations for deeper values, her mental capacities, her essential womanhood, her love of country, of people and of her son. She always said what she thought was right or true, with no fear of the person to whom she was speaking. Sonja might be fearful of riding on a roller-coaster or stepping onto an escalator, but she could confront a secret police agent or an important personality without flinching.

When I first met her on the shores of the blue Adriatic Sea, she was a Yugoslav. But what would she be now, as her mother was Bosnian and her father Montenegrin, after the break-up of the old nation in tragic circumstances? Aurelia, her mother, was an artist and a descendant of the medieval Tvrtko royal dynasty, whose coat of arms was for a time that of today's Bosnian state – a deep blue background with golden fleurs-de-lys and a white diagonal. Her father was a soldier, a colonel in the old Royal Serbian Army.

I still have a photograph of him, resplendent in his dress uniform. He liked good-looking women, and he fell in love with the aristocratic beauty of Aurelia. They had one child, called Sonja by her mother, and Zivka by her father. I always supposed that this was the same name, one being of Catholic usage and the other of Serbian Orthodox origin. Sonja was a teenager before her parents were officially married and she attended their wedding. Her family situation was enlivened by the existence of two half-sisters, one from her father's first marriage and the other from an unpublicised liaison of her mother's. But no brothers.

As soldiers move around and the camp followers with them, Sonja was born in Negotin on the Bulgarian frontier, something of a garrison town. However, the presence of a child could have been a restriction to the lifestyle of her parents, and she was eventually sent to stay with some distant relatives in Jagodin, now called Svetozarevo. It is in the heart of Serbia, an agricultural town famous for its Gavrilovic dried sausages.

Perhaps the family with whom she stayed were related to her father, as both their surnames were Aleksić. Her childhood was spent with them until she became a student in Belgrade many years later.

In Jagodin all writing was in the cyrillic script and people were brought up in the Orthodox faith. The memory of nearly four centuries of Turkish occupation was still strong in people's minds and, in the face of oppression, the priests had played a key role in maintaining their belief in God, their nationhood and themselves. In spite of her mixed parentage, at heart Sonja was a Serb. Her deepest cultural roots were in the soil of that area.

After our war experiences we were both searching for a destiny. At that moment neither had a known future, a secure career, a home to go to, a safe job waiting to be picked up, a supporting wider family. And yet, one day about a year later, after civil and religious wedding procedures, we stepped onto a train in Rijeka station and began an uncharted journey together.

Even before we were married I was gaining some inkling of dramatic events in Sonja's life. She told me of her time in a concentration camp and of her clash with the authorities when Tito to came to power and Yugoslavia was a Communist dictatorship. During the early days of our marriage as I listened to her, sometimes for hours, I began to know the full amazing story.

Sonja had been sentenced to death by both the Communists and the Nazis and had yet survived the hostile impact of those two powerful forces of the 20th century. When Hitler's army invaded her country the young King Peter defied his advisors who were recommending surrender. He called for resistance and Sonja was among the thousands of Belgrade students who demonstrated support for him in the streets. It was all in vain and the Nazi troops flooded across Croatia and the Danube Plain and entered the capital. King Peter sought refuge in

Britain, but the students stayed behind, smarting from the treachery of earlier leaders and the shame of defeat. Sonja was just 18 years old and she made contact with the growing resistance movement of Tito, whose real name was Josip Broz, and who had been well-trained in Communism during several periods in Moscow. She became a message carrier for his intelligence network.

In 1942 she was captured and spent the next three years in a concentration camp in Serbia, run by the Germans. In 1944 the war was moving increasingly against the Axis Powers and the camp commandant sentenced many of the women prisoners to death. The women would be lined up and one day those whose names began with D would be called out, bunched together and taken away to be shot; another day it would be the 12 women on the right; the next time those with dark brown hair, and so on. Sonja wondered when her turn would come. The Red Army reached the Yugoslav border and panic began to set in amongst the German guards. In the confusion Sonja and some of her fellow inmates escaped. They made their way back to Belgrade and were there when the city was liberated.

Sonja, now 22, was able to resume her law studies and become qualified. She also had a gift for languages. When I met her she spoke eight: Serbo-Croat, Bulgarian, Russian, English, French, Spanish, Italian and German and wrote in the cyrillic and latin scripts. This led her into contact with foreign diplomats and others who were again able to set foot in the country. The fact that she played three musical instruments, the piano, the violin and the classical guitar, enhanced the attractiveness of her personality.

When Tito came to power, the local Communist leadership quickly realised Sonja's potential and began to pressure her to become a party activist. She wanted greater social justice and was deeply concerned about the reconstruction of her country, but her independent spirit reacted against the pressures of the apparatchiks and she resisted them. The upshot was that she was arrested and charged with being 'an enemy of the people', given a summary trial and again sentenced to death. She was sent to a camp where sentences of death were carried out by shooting at 3 o'clock in the morning. The time came when she was told that she would be executed the following morning. She got dressed before midnight, tried to look as tidy as possible and prepared her mind for death. No one came for her. The same thing happened for nine nights running and in her mind she died nine times. On the tenth morning she was called into the commandant's office, told that there had been a mistake, and put out onto the street.

Why was she treated in this way and then released without any explanation? Was it to give her such a fright that she would then keep quiet and toe the line? Was it because some senior person intervened at a high level, for example her brother-in-law who had been Tito's doctor, or did the camp commandant have a stroke of conscience? Sonja always felt that it was thanks to a Jew who was a fellow prisoner in the German camp, who also survived and later became an official in Belgrade's city government – and had protested to higher authorities when he heard of Sonja's intended fate. To survive such an experience without bitterness, to keep an open heart and a positive and cheerful outlook is a triumph of the human spirit. To live beside such a woman, through thick and thin, for nearly 30 years was the deepest experience of my life.

To Sonja

on her Saint's Day (St Michael and All Angels)

Out of the sunshine and the blue sky
    Out of the sandy shore and the clear sea
Out of the dangers of a fighting past
    Out of the mysteries of a troubled age

An arrow flew straight to my heart
>   Flecked with chestnut and hazel colours
Barbed with southern Slavonic charm
>   Strong as the open heart of a Serb
Light as the memory of a smile
>   Clean as the joy of a child at play
I fell forever a victim of the bow
>   That hurls the darts of Cupid to the winds
So that I sang, so that I cried
>   And loved to live with Sonja at my side.

———— ❦ ————

After that first visit, I had to return to England, but I left my heart behind. And within months, I was back. Soon I was fortunate enough to visit her Uncle Peter and his wife, who had brought Sonja up as a child and they gave me a heart-warming welcome. The wife was a marvellous cook and prepared particularly lovely *sarma*, fresh cabbage leaves stuffed with mince and rice and herbs and prepared in a delicious sauce. It was with a mixture of pride and shame, that I ate twelve of those succulent creations. This act of gourmandise spread around the town and I was acclaimed as the champion sarma eater of Svetozarevo. This was a plus point locally and seemed to shatter the image of the stuffy Englishman. There is a horrible pun lurking there – the stuffy Englishman who stuffed himself with the stuffed *sarma*.

The local mayor at that time was alarmed to have an unknown foreigner in his community and would not let me stay with the family friends. Instead I was parked in a roughish hotel, so that the authorities could keep an eye on me.

One evening we went to the popular Saturday dance in a big café, where I was taught the traditional steps, always to very repetitive music, a bit like today's rap. But it was a cheerful atmosphere and seemed to release some of the tensions of police-state life.

We visited the grave of a relative in the cemetery on the hillside just outside the town. A feature of a Serbian Orthodox cemetery is that the gravestones have flat table-like tops. And I was told that this was done deliberately for visitors to be able to eat something during visits, which we did to the accompaniment of a few tears from Sonja.

One day when taking everyone out for a drive, we came to a crossing on the main railway line from Belgrade to Macedonia and Greece. Without the slightest concern I drove across the line at a good speed to the horrified shouts of Uncle Peter and the near panic of his wife. 'What's the matter?' I asked. 'Don't you realise?' he said, 'we could have been hit by a train, because the gates don't work properly and the train drivers don't care who they run over.' I was more careful after that!

Many times I would listen to Sonja for hours telling me the events of her life, particularly of the years spent in the concentration camp. She would say to me, 'What do you think the women talked about most? Sex? No, food! We would describe beautiful meals that we had eaten and wonderful dishes that we had prepared. We would go over recipes and recall fruits and vegetables from our gardens, I would remember my guardians' vineyard in deepest Serbia with the stream running through it, and the picnics of grilled meat and *cevapcici*, the Yugoslavian skinless sausage of pork, veal and lamb. The fresh fruit from the orchard, and the local salami, which was quite famous, eaten with crusty bread straight from the oven and gorgeous farm butter. The hard, white cheese with a clean, nutty taste, and abundant salads of fresh sliced onions, crisp lettuce and luscious, strongly-flavoured tomatoes.'

It makes me think of the one time that I was really ill during my travels throughout Serbia with Sonja. We were driving one day from Svetozarevo to Belgrade and we stopped on the outskirts at the hillside cemetery to remember a long lost friend. There we ate a slice of bread and a tasty tomato. We had been driving along quiet, country roads for about an hour, when we slowed down behind a horse-drawn cart filled with gleaming, multi-shaped, glorious deep red tomatoes. I drew up in front of the cart to admire the farmer's crop and Sonja told him how impressed I was and how much I loved the fruit. His response was typical of the natural, generous heart of the Serbian countryman. He filled a large bag with 20 to 30 tomatoes and handed it to me. I offered to pay, but he rejected it. It was satisfaction enough for him to give pleasure to someone who admired the results of his skill and labour.

I gorged myself during the next hour which led to a very painful, stomach blockage. I was only just able to reach the house of friends with whom we were staying without collapsing. I rolled around in pain on a hard bed and finally went to sleep for many hours. I awoke feeling fine and fresh, as though nothing had happened.

I was now on a grand tour of Sonja's friends and relatives, whilst waiting for the various consular and ecclesiastical permissions needed for our marriage. Although it was winter, it was a kindly one and I had bought a warm, second-hand overcoat in London that served me well. Sonja did not much like my wearing what had been someone else's garment and she rather pointedly bought me a new suit and a splendid Homburg hat when we reached Zagreb, the capital of Croatia. In Zagreb we met her half-sister, whose husband had a photographic business and who took some nice engagement pictures.

Sonja had an old friend who was a poet and she arranged for us to have coffee with him in a rather dingy bar. It turned out that he was not well-viewed by the regime and was living a very precarious existence. His work was not published and he received no help from the state. I asked him how he survived. He said, 'In the summer I stand at the entrance of the Cathedral and when I see a German tourist with a camera about to enter, I say to him in an official manner that it is not permitted to take cameras inside. They ask me to hold their camera whilst they look around, and as soon as they are within, I scoot off to the local camera shop and sell them for a bargain price. That keeps me going during the tourist season.' Having digested this unusual way of survival I then asked him how he managed during the winter. 'Well,' he replied, 'then I get myself declared insane, and am looked after in the local asylum.'

When we arrived in Belgrade, we met Sonja's half-brother-in-law, Lubomir Rašović, who had been Tito's doctor during and after wartime resistance. Eventually he was rewarded for keeping the great man in good shape by being made Dean of Belgrade University's Faculty of Medicine, a position from which he had just retired when we met. He was an impressive man and a very good surgeon, had attended numerous international medical events and been given many medals and honours in the process. He was a sincere believer in Communism and thought that it was the only way to bring justice and plenty for all.

Many years later when the Berlin Wall fell and Soviet Russia disintegrated he was totally dismayed. He felt that his life had been wasted and his dreams shattered and he died very shortly afterwards.

His wife, Desa, Sonja's half-sister, was a strong and handsome woman and shared her husband's views. They were both Montenegrins and I came to the conclusion that they were rather like the Scots in London, holding many of the top jobs in politics and business.

For a few days we stayed with an old friend of Sonja, a poorly paid journalist with a one-room flat. So we slept on the floor in the kitchen and the four of us led a convivial collective existence in about 20 square metres, which was nothing compared with the numbers in some of the overcrowded Indian homes that I had known.

At that time most of the Belgrade shops were state run and looked very dull, although café life was quite lively. During the journey I was becoming used to frequent *slivović* (plum brandy) drams and Turkish coffees (sweet and strong in small cups) as offered by every friend we met and every home we visited. I must have a strong resistance to alcohol and an efficient digestive system, as somehow I survived all these excesses.

We had a memorable visit to the National War Memorial at Avala on a wooded hill outside the city. Dropping off a bus we began to walk through the forest, when I was sufficiently overcome by the desire for immortality to stop by a large tree and carve our two-initialled hearts pierced together by an arrow. Near the top of the hill was a battered area where a passenger aeroplane had flown into the slopes killing all aboard. We paid homage at the War Memorial and enjoyed the vast view across the plains of Serbia.

Another tourist visit was to the fortress of Kalimegdan which commands the junction of the great rivers Danube and Sava. It is quite a defensive and architectural achievement, which provides both a romantic and awesome ambiance.

We flew from Belgrade to Sarajevo, a short trip over the Javor Mountains landing, as usual, at an airport some distance from the city. Sarajevo is in a beautiful setting clustered around a riverbed and, on its adjacent slopes, surrounded by an impressive circle of low mountains. This site was later to make it very vulnerable to artillery and sniper fire in the shameful siege and semi-destruction of a wonderful architectural heritage during the Bosnian conflict of 1992 to 1995.

We stayed at a small old hotel in the centre, close to the narrow streets lined by shops and cafés. There was a place in one of the squares where you could see a mosque, a Catholic cathedral, a synagogue and an Orthodox church at a sweeping glance. This typified the open and respectful tradition of this noble city, which for hundreds of years had shown tolerance to the worshippers of all faiths.

I was breath-taken, in the market place, by the mountains of cabbages and the variety of colourful vegetables and fruits brought in, mostly by horse and donkey-drawn carts, from the farms in the surrounding valleys. I did a double-take when I saw the local buses. They were old London double-deckers, doubtless sold off cheaply after the war, and were logically called *Londonats*. We travelled out on them to spots of interest in the suburbs.

My mother-in-law to be came from Sarajevo. She was a descendant of the Royal Dynasty of Tvrtko, which had ruled Bosnia in the Middle Ages. I once asked a Bosnian friend about the origins of the noble families. 'Oh,' he said, 'They were the best sheep stealers of their day.' But Aurelia Branković, for that was her name, was very aristocratic and would not get out of a car until someone opened the door for her. She was an academy painter and was also a costumier and scene designer for the Yugoslav National Theatre. In a Communist society everyone had to have a job. She was also an expert on national costume and gave me a book of her sketches of the different regional styles.

Fortunately she rather liked me. Her idea of an Englishman had been a weedy individual with a straggly moustache and she was pleasantly surprised when her daughter's predilection turned out to be rather well-built and cleanshaven. I suppose that in the Balkan tradition, if a man had a moustache it would be sizeable and greatly admired. So, better to have no moustache at all, than a miserable excuse for one.

Aurelia was Roman Catholic. She was always very nervous about her aristocratic background in case it jeopardised her chance to work in a state-controlled system. Sonja, who I suppose could have claimed to be a princess, never made anything of it and was more identified with her father's humbler Montenegrin origins. She also accepted his Orthodox faith.

We took the train from Sarajevo to Dubrovnik, a medieval

12. Sonja's father

13. Sonja's mother

14. Sonja, 1939

15. Rijeka and
Kvarner Bay

16. Our engagement,
1961

17. The
Orthodox
marriage
ceremony,
Rijeka

18. Sonja with granddaughter Natalie

19. With son, Frederick

20. Sonja's funeral, 1990

21. With Natalie at Caux, 1999

22. Wedding of Natalie and Jabez, Melbourne, March 2002

walled city on the blue Adriatic Sea. An enthralling journey along steep valleys, through mountain passes and following river beds. A highlight was the halt at Mostar, a mixed Moslem-Croat city, whose two communities lived on opposite sides of the River Drina. They were linked by a remarkable single-span, almost semi-circular bridge, built in the Middle Ages, and for which the town was renowned. One could not have imagined then that this bridge, a symbol of communal harmony, would be destroyed during the recent conflict. It has since been rebuilt and may again become a source of unity. The vineyards around Mostar produced a very good white wine, *Zilavka*, and I recalled that this was the first wine that I bought to share with Sonja in the restaurant on top of the Neboder skyscraper hotel in Rijeka.

A dramatic incident occurred at the station, as I was taken ill with a mixture of poisoning and flu and, completely knocked-out. I lay across the seats in the compartment. People arrived who wanted to sit in those places, but Sonja resisted them with vigour. Then the train conductor arrived and again Sonja refused to let anyone disturb me. Finally a local official turned up to demand that I resume a single seat. He threatened Sonja with arrest and punishment, but she would not budge. Finally, the passengers, the conductor and the official admitted defeat and left us in peace. It was my first, but not the last, example of Sonja courageously standing up to Communist officialdom and winning the day.

We stayed in Dubrovnik at the port just outside the walled city. The town was built by the Italians in the Middle Ages in gleaming white stone. The walls completely surround the city with magnificent views across the Adriatic and on the land side to the distant mountains. It is the only example that I know of a city that had completely preserved its original buildings. One evening we saw a Shakespeare play performed in a natural setting, as the bard might have imagined it. The beauty of the buildings provided realistic scenery.

To return to Rijeka we took the coastal tourist boat with a pleasant but not very roomy cabin. This is the best way to experience the sea and islands of the Adriatic. I remember sighting the island of Korcula through a light morning mist and admiring the town and harbour as they came closer and closer. The boat called at the ports of the larger islands and I recall that one of them, I think it was Brac, promised visitors some of their money back if the sun did not shine every day that they were there. I suppose that the local weathermen must have worked out the odds rather carefully.

Sonja lived in a mansard apartment, an attic under the roof. It was at the top of a six-story building and involved climbing many stairs. It had one room and a kitchen. Because of her non-compromising stance with the authorities she had been moved out of a spacious apartment and allocated more humble premises, doubtless also as a lesson to others, *pour encourager les autres*, as the French express it.

In Rijeka, we went for long walks along the coast towards the south along a promontory and down to a small town with worn-out boats anchored in the bay. On the way, there was a small privately owned café that specialised in a dish of fresh sardines, large sliced onion rings and a little lettuce or sweet peppers. We had some good talks there. But once, out of the blue, she said, 'Well, if you are not sure about us, end it now with no hard feelings.' I didn't want to end it, and the thought made me more resolute.

She was a fair player and wanted to be sure that we were on solid ground with our relationship. For both of us it was meant to be an endplay and not an experimental foray. If we made a decision now it was for life, no matter what storms and disappointments might befall. We also knew that we had to keep on trying, that marriage was a beginning and a journey not an arrival, and that our care for one another would always triumph over our misunderstandings and disagreements. Reticent though I am to give advice to others, I would say to young couples that your first collision is not a fatal accident and that total repair is always possible.

Further down the coast was Crikvenica, reputed to have the finest scampi in the world, and I would testify to that. In the other direction towards the Istrian peninsula we swam at a fine beach, which I recall mostly for the hundreds of tiny shrimps that tried to eat the hairs on my legs, doing no more harm than causing a strong tickling sensation. It was close to a naval training establishment and once when I took a picture of sailor recruits, rowing in a long wooden boat, a nearby guard confiscated the film in my camera and warned me against taking pictures of naval installations.

Another example of state control was when we were in the local butcher's shop and a big consignment of meat was delivered to him from the nearby abattoir. The butcher protested that it was far more than he would ever sell and the driver replied, 'That is what it has been decided that you should get and it is your duty to sell it.' No argument! I did get to like the local *pershut*, a very tasty dried ham. It went very well after *gibanica*, a flaky pastry cheese pie. I must admit that I like food and have enjoyed a wide variety in every country that I have visited.

Since my wife died I have made some efforts to learn to cook, but without real success. Sonja had never liked me in the kitchen, saying that I was in the way and very slow, that it even took me two hours to prepare a dish of cold meats! I thought that stock was something you bought and sold on the Stock Exchange. Weights and measures were a mystery to me, and what was a casserole? However, I eventually found a book called *How to Boil an Egg*, which assumed no previous knowledge. For example, 'To boil an egg, you must first buy some eggs in a shop, making sure that they are fresh. Then you fill a pan with water, heat it to boiling point and then carefully drop in the eggs, leaving them for between four and five minutes depending on whether you prefer them soft or hard.'

In France I am saved from starvation by the selection of ready-cooked dishes that butchers, *charcutiers* and *traiteurs* have on sale each day. I make my choice and then I just have to heat them up in a casserole, now that I know what that receptacle is. And the *pâtissiers* always have a tempting choice of fruit pies and chocolate cakes.

Starting out together

Our wedding was on 17 January 1962 and we had an Orthodox Church wedding for which the Patriarch in Belgrade had
given permission. The civil wedding took place earlier in the
day, which in Yugoslavia was the legal occasion. It was in
Rijeka Town Hall and conducted by a civic official. The state
also provided an official translator in order to be quite sure
that I knew what I was letting myself in for. One of the principal points was that from then on all our worldly goods
would be split on a fifty-fifty basis. As all that I owned at that
time could be put into two suitcases, one of them with me, and
the other in storage in London, I was not against an equal
sharing of present and future accumulations of wealth.

The thought of taking on to live with another person for the
rest of my life was bearing in on me and I had been drinking
vinjak, the local brandy, like water. However, come the day, I
thought, well you have to be sporting and you are going to go
through with it, so relax. I think that Sonja was more on edge
than I was until all the ceremonies were over. But she looked
marvellous and I had no regrets.

During the wedding the official kept making sure that I was
fully aware of the gravity of my commitment. This accounts
for the fact that, in the photograph of us leaving, friends tell
me that I look like a Member of Parliament who has just lost
the election.

The marriage in the little Rijeka Orthodox Church was
another matter. Sonja had one bridesmaid of about her age,
but in accordance with custom I had two best men. They were

enormous Macedonians, married to friends of Sonja, and they towered above me on either side. In the photographs it looks as though I am being forced through a shotgun wedding.

The service was rather like taking part in an opera. We both wore crowns and held a candle in each hand. I kept dropping candle wax on the priest's robe as we moved around the church according to the ritual. The singing of the choir was beautiful, especially the deep bass voices. I was told afterwards that the bride always tries to stand on the bridegroom's feet during the service and, if successful, she will be boss in the home. I don't know if Sonja tried, but, in the event I think that neither of us was the boss, more like a well-fought draw.

After the ceremony we drove high into the nearby mountains to a privately run restaurant and ate local dried ham, roast lamb and fresh salad, and drank sparkling *biser* wine, for the wedding feast. Stretching before us was a panoramic view of the Adriatic Sea and the nearby islands.

A few weeks before the marriage, I had received a disturbing call from the Consul General to say that my wife could be prevented from leaving the country with me. I told him that that would defeat the object of the exercise and could he do anything to help. He rang back a few days later and said that he thought he had solved the problem. He had read the Yugoslav law about marriage and there was a clause that said that a married woman should be allowed to accompany her husband wherever he went. He would ensure that the authorities at the frontier had this information and ask them to allow Sonja to travel with me without let or hindrance. When we left several days later by the Orient Express, the Yugoslav police at the frontier examined our passports with great care, referred them to their officer and he must have had the message, because we went safely through to Trieste in Italy. I hold my diplomatic service in high esteem because of their intelligent handling of what could have been a major problem.

The first dramatic moment after marriage was our arrival in

Venice Station, where there was a halt of ten minutes or so. I took this as my opportunity to go to the station bookstall to buy a London newspaper. It took me longer than expected and I returned to the carriage with only a minute or two to spare before departure. Sonja was in a great state of distress, almost in tears. She must have been thinking that this perfidious Englishman had already given her the slip and she would be left stranded in a foreign land. I did my best to comfort her, but it took an hour or two into the journey to Milan for her to recover. Lesson number one for an untrained husband – do not leave your new wife alone during stops at stations. Take her with you or stay put.

I had arranged for our honeymoon to stay with friends in Lausanne and then in Paris. For a start I did not have the money for even reasonably priced hotels, but I really wanted to show off my bride to two very close old friends and their wives. It was a good move because they all took to Sonja. One of them even said in French, '*Tu as trouvé une femme épatante.*' (You have found a fantastic wife).

Our Lausanne friends were Bernard and Martine Golay, whom I had known for about 20 years. He had been a highly skilled watchmaker, producing a prize-winning extra-flat watch, and he now had his own company for time-keeping equipment and printed circuits. His wife taught English at the university.

In Paris we stayed with Maurice Mercier, the trade unionist, who had become a very close friend, and his wife, Lina. I particularly remember a Marseillaise bouillabaisse meal at a local restaurant. For the uninitiated that is a luscious Mediterranean fish soup, but closer to a stew, made from several varieties of fish and shelled seafood. Maurice and Sonja reminisced about their wartime resistance experiences and gained a great respect for one another. Many years later, at their suggestion, we bought a second home in southwest France close to Cahors where they had retired to.

Neither Sonja nor I had more than a few pounds in our pockets, perhaps £50 in my bank account, no jobs to go to and no place to live in Britain. The whole thing was crazy. When we reached Victoria Station in London, we took a cab to a cheap hotel in Bayswater where I had once stayed and booked in. Walking around the streets in the coming days, we found a room on the top floor of a six-storey apartment house in Kensington Gardens Square at a very low rent and moved in there. I recovered my suitcase from storage and wrote to a magazine that had not paid me for an article. I was relieved to get £12 by return post. It is hard to believe that 20 years later, I would be among Britain's best-paid publishers.

A few weeks after arriving in London I asked Sonja what she thought about living in another country. 'It is more like being on another planet,' was her reply.

The flat where we lived involved climbing up five flights of stairs, and the lavatory was a couple of floors below. A previous occupant must have always let his cigarettes burn themselves out when he put them on the mantelpiece or the table, because both items were lined with burn marks, but as beggars we could not be choosers. I thought that it was my duty to carry the heavy shopping up those stairs, which I did, but Sonja would never allow me to carry it in public. It puzzled me, because Sonja was a sophisticated, talented, highly educated lawyer and, in a Western context, would not have been expected to perform such tasks without the man's involvement.

In later years when we entertained friends or business guests for dinner, she would wait on everyone throughout the meal and only come and sit with us for coffee. Of course, they always protested, but she could not be moved, saying that was her family custom. She confided in me that it gave her the possibility of doing the washing-up as the meal went along and so she was completely relaxed to join us at the end with no more work to do.

My marriage was by way of being a package deal, because Sonja already had a six-year old son called Frederick. For some months after we left Rijeka he stayed with a family friend, but we wanted him to join us as soon as we could accommodate him. Eventually our landlady agreed to find him a small room in the basement and he joined us. Then began a process of adoption. In Britain, a child of his age has to agree to being adopted in front of the local Children's Officer. Fred said yes and so I became a father and I have looked on Fred as my own son since then. We never had a child of our own, but did not feel frustrated because of that.

Fred had inherited some of the artistic talents of his Bosnian grandmother and one year won the first prize for school art for the whole of England. I was always disappointed that he did not take it up as a career, but he studied restaurant and hotel keeping, taking a Westminster College course and working as a *commis* in the Wig and Pen Club in Fleet Street.

Later things went wrong with his various business endeavours, but, no matter what, he was always ready to try again. He was gifted mechanically, loved cars and motorbikes, and at one time he helped to run a service team for Formula One Motorbike racing. He was always attractive to the girls and at the early age of 17 fell for and married Jacqueline, a good-looking Bunny Girl and model. She became the mother of Natalie, my beloved granddaughter.

During our first summer, to supplement my precarious freelance earnings, I did some weeks as a courier for a travel company on the Continent. It was hard to be separated, but perhaps it prepared us for travels abroad during my publishing career. At the same time Sonja became friendly with our landlady, a plump and smart Irish woman, married to a much older wartime Polish refugee, who had made enough money to buy the hotel property. Sonja earned some money as her assistant, looking after the guests and being generally helpful, and working hard in keeping the rooms tidy. She was also looking after Fred, who on arrival spoke only Serbo-Croat, but still had to attend the local primary school. Amazingly, in about three months he was speaking quite fluent English. Fred would then become very cross if his mother spoke Serbo-Croat to him in the street and insisted that she speak in English. In later years when we took him with us on visits to Yugoslavia, he then spoke his old language with an English accent, which caused high amusement.

We found a two-bedroom flat to rent in Clarendon Road at the dividing line between the bourgeois and the workers' areas of North Kensington. It was on the ground floor and I had the occupancy of a small back garden if I looked after it, which I managed to do. This seemed like heaven – to have a wife, a son, a home and a job. Our incomes were supplemented by my freelance writing and Sonja did translation for a legal firm near the office where I worked close to the Law Courts. At last this enabled her to buy some decent clothes: she had a great dress sense and looked sensationally smart. She also improved my sartorial appearance!

About three years later, when I had managed to save a little in my bank account, we were at a sale in the local big store and wandered into the fur department. Perhaps this had been plotted earlier, if you believe in conspiracy theories, but one of the saleswomen showed us a splendid mink coat. It fitted Sonja perfectly and she looked magnificent in it. It was going for what was described as the bargain price of £1,300 – just the amount of my bank balance. To me this was a huge sum and I had never spent such an amount at one go in my life. But it clearly meant everything to Sonja to own a real fur coat as good as this one. So I melted and, with tears in my eyes of concern not joy, I signed away my small savings.

When I look back it seems a small sum. But to me it was a watershed between thinking of money as something to accumulate and something to spend on making life more pleasant. Sonja hung onto that coat until it was stolen 20 years later from our Knightsbridge flat. I hope that someone else got as much out of it as she did. When you think of it, it only cost me £65 a year!

Fred went to the local Church of England school and was enrolled in the church choir. It turned out that the priest in charge was fond of boys, which was a revelation when Fred told me about it. Today, paedophilia is a major crime, yet in those days it was hardly known and certainly not a matter of public concern. Fortunately Fred managed to keep the man at a distance. It also turned out that Fred was quite a wheeler-dealer in exchanging his possessions for better ones with the other boys. So much so that one evening an irate parent rang our bell to demand the return of a valuable object that his son had given to Fred in exchange for some worthless item.

A short time after our settling down in our own flat, Sonja's mother, Aurelia, came to stay with us for about six weeks. As she was a painter, she decided to create as many pictures as possible for our home, as a belated wedding present. When I discovered the cost of paint, canvases and equipment I was, at first, very circumspect on the matter, but ever since I have been grateful for her legacy of more than 20 pictures which have adorned and enlightened the many homes in which we have lived.

Aurelia was not in good health, so we took her to be examined by our local General Practitioner who had been recommended by my celebrated cardiologist uncle, Sir John Parkinson, pioneer of the electro-cardiogram. The GP was direct-speaking and had once told me not to waste his time with trivial complaints. He was helpful and considerate with my mother-in-law, but, as she was not on his list, he sent in a bill. It was Sonja's habit always to bargain, a sensible Balkan trait, when buying in the shops and she was often successful in getting reductions. Thinking that the doctor's bill was rather heavy, she decided, to my alarm, to debate it with him. It had never crossed my mind that one might bargain over a doctor's fee, but she did and, lo and behold, he cut it in half. It made me reflect, with thankfulness, how much money she must have saved me during those early months of marriage.

I learned something from Aurelia about what it is to be a true artist. I had asked her to paint the portrait of a senior business colleague. She had several sittings and worked hard at it in oils. But somehow there was always an unpleasant sneer on his features, which was not apparent on looking at him. It must have represented some inner defect in his character that communicated itself to the artist and which she had to interpret in her work. Even the final version, which was perfect in portraying his general appearance, dress and office background, carried in his features a rather malicious expression. I am told that, after he had thanked her for the picture, he took it immediately to an attic and that it was never seen again. He must have seen his true self in the portrait.

Crisis and Happiness with Sonja

It is hard to include the following experience in my story. Particularly as I was the principal culprit. We had been married about eight years and were both in our forties when lightning struck. The top and bottom of the matter was that I had begun what I thought was a trivial flirtation with one of the ladies in the office. How commonplace can you get? I don't think that Sonja was aware of it and, if she was by instinct, if not by knowledge, she did not bring it up with me.

At that time her mother died and she went to Yugoslavia for the funeral and to deal with the consequences. Whilst she was away the young lady in question invited me to her flat for dinner and, foolishly, I accepted. Intimacy took place and in typical male style I hoped that would be the end of the matter, but that was not the view of the lady. Knowing that she had me at a disadvantage, she made a real set at me.

Under this pressure, I began to behave with Sonja in what she must have divined as a guilty fashion. Then one night, sitting comfortably at home in our Wimbledon flat, she confronted me with her suspicions. Perhaps I should have denied that anything was amiss. Afterwards several people told me I should have done. However I played the card of admitting what I considered to be more of a misdemeanour than a sin in the hope that she would be understanding and forgiving – a lot to ask. She was heartbroken. In her earlier days, before our marriage, perhaps she had not always been without blame in these matters, but with me she had decided to play straight and be a devoted and faithful wife. She wept and she was angry. Thus began four years when our marriage hung in the balance.

Perhaps Sonja had thought that an Englishman's word was his bond, that I would take a more serious view of loyalty than her own countrymen, whom she considered to be unfaithful by nature. But she did suspect that I might be an easy catch for a determined female approach, having seen me wilt a little in the presence of predatory beauties. For this reason she feared that I had fallen in love with this woman and that I planned to divorce her and leave her and Fred. My protests that this was not the case did not convince her for a long time. She told me later that she had got in touch with friends in Europe to try to make arrangements to leave Britain and complete Fred's education somewhere else.

At this time I was rising rapidly in my work, had left one company for a more senior position in another and was setting up a new publishing imprint for a major multinational in Britain. Sometimes I would leave my office to go to a public telephone box and talk to Sonja in efforts to convince her that I still loved her and nobody else. At other times during the weekends I would drive her out of London to go for long walks in the woods and try to persuade her not to leave me. But she always had a meal ready for me when I returned from the office and we still slept in the same bed. In her there must have been a lot of deeply hurt Balkan pride. The southern Slavs had lived through a chequered history and for centuries suffered defeats, occupations and treacheries, whilst in Britain no one had trodden on us for hundreds of years. She must have felt cornered in an alien land at the mercy of an unreliable man.

Why did we not call it a day? One reason for me was that I had sworn vows and made a commitment at the marriage ceremony that was for life. I still had a deep respect for such an undertaking. My father had taught me to promise nothing that I did not intend to fulfil. I was going to hang in there and persist in finding a way through. There was also a wider family tradition and, among my numerous relatives, I only knew of one case where a marriage had broken down. Perhaps I also felt that divorce would be a black mark on my professional career, although I had once been lunched at the Ritz by a Chairman to tell me that he thought that I would go further in life if I divorced my outspoken wife. She must have upset him at some time with a well-directed shaft! I can only surmise why Sonja did not just walk out on me.

When we were back again on an even keel, she never discussed it. Perhaps she loved my good points more than she was put off by my bad ones. The fact is, I don't really know, but there finally came a day when we were on firm ground again. She was able to forgive me, and from then on our marriage got better and better and it was at a high point many years later in the months before she died.

Sonja was an interesting mixture of the aristocrat from her mother's side and the earthy soldier from her Montenegrin father. Both strains seemed to harmonise in a refreshing directness, which either carried a direct punch or a delayed depth charge. I shall never forget our first meeting with the mayor of the town where we were living at the time. I was rather keen that we should become friendly with him and at last the opportunity arose. We were introduced to him at a public reception. Sonja had been reading the local paper in which the mayor's picture appeared quite frequently and she said spontaneously to him, 'You look much more handsome in your photographs than you do in reality.' Normally never lost for words, this completely silenced him, and I muttered a few niceties and slunk away dragging Sonja with me.

On the way home I was really cross and asked her if she thought that that was the best way to start a friendship. 'Don't worry,' she said, 'he has a very strong personality and when he thinks about it he will know that my remark was true.' Still fuming I dropped the subject. However, she must have been right because in the event we developed a good relationship with the mayor, and he was always very helpful to us.

We frequently entertained my business friends and acquaintances at home or in restaurants, and Sonja was always completely and naturally outspoken with them. Afterwards I would often say, 'How could you say such a thing to him?' 'Well, it was true.' 'But it's not because something is true that people are going to like it.' 'Well, we'll see.' In 20 years of this kind of contact I can only remember one occasion when a person took great exception to something that she said. And I thought he was asking for it anyway, by more or less accusing her, as a Sarajevan, of being responsible for starting the First World War. After her death, many of those who had been in her verbal firing line wrote to me to say how much they had benefited from her honesty and that they knew it always came from a caring heart.

Shortly after settling down in London she decided to join the Conservative Party, which I had never done, still holding fond memories of my left-wing student days and having voted for a Labour government after the war. 'Why?' I asked her. She replied, 'Well, I just want to get as far as I can away from my experience of Communism, and this is one way that I can do that.' She did door-to-door work in the poorest part of the constituency. To the people in the workers' blocks she seemed to be some kind of phenomenon. How could someone from Communist Yugoslavia go round actively supporting the Tories? But they loved her spirit as did the Conservative candidate, of course. He later became a cabinet minister and a European Commissioner.

Travelling on the Continent, we often stayed at a beautiful converted-mill hotel. Then came the day when I stayed there alone after her death. When I was having breakfast on the balcony overlooking the millstream, one of the chambermaids sought me out, having heard of my loss. 'I wanted you to know,' she said, 'that your wife was the nicest person who ever stayed in this hotel. She always treated me as an equal human being, listened to me and helped me with my problems.' I was overcome and shed some tears. Sonja was one person; she did not try to be all things to all men; she was what she was. She really cared for people, and their social position was not a factor. For some reason, she was incapable of not saying what she thought. This was very good for a reserved Englishman who would rather say nothing than upset a relationship, particularly if his own self-interest might be in question. Perhaps also, if you have survived three years in a concentration camp, beating about the bush, putting on a false front or trying to impress are just ridiculous, meaningless attitudes.

Shortly after we were married, I noticed that she would always put a piece of uneaten bread from a restaurant or even from a friend's home into her handbag. One day, when she left her handbag on the chair and was out of the room, I surreptitiously looked into it. Sure enough there were a number of dry crusts at the bottom. When she came back I told her what I had done and asked her why. 'It goes back to the days of war and especially the concentration camp, when every morsel of food stood between us and starvation and I gained a great respect for each crumb. Ever since then I have never been able to throw food away, even if it is just to keep it to give to the birds later.'

When we went to America she rather liked the idea of the doggy bag to take food home from the restaurant. She became very persistent about it with London restaurants, who were not accustomed to this practice.

She decided that the Ritz in London was wrong to print the dishes on the menu in French with an English translation underneath. She felt that in London it should be the other way round. She always rubbed this in with the restaurant manager and even made friends with the Director's mother to exert more pressure. I told her that this was ridiculous, but I had to eat humble pie when she took me to the restaurant one day and, lo and behold, English came first on the menu followed by a French translation.

She was also a gifted musician. Even though very out of practice, she could sit down at any piano and play a decent tune, or strum on a guitar. On one occasion we were in a continental restaurant with a violinist visiting the tables and playing for the guests. When he reached our table Sonja let him play a few notes and then she took over his violin and finished the piece, to my amazement and the applause of the diners. She loved opera and in London was a keen 'Friend of Covent Garden'.

Occasionally Sonja did not get it right and I recall when one of my farming cousins, David Porter, with whom we were staying in Herefordshire, produced a beautiful, freshly-fished, River Wye salmon for dinner. When asked how she liked it she said, 'Well, it just tasted like fish,' to the disappointment of my cousin, who had expected more fulsome praise. Then there was the occasion when she was the hostess at a publishing reception and popped an olive into a senior American's malt whisky to his complete horror. Unabashed she fished it out and brought him another malt. She had mistakenly thought that if olives were good enough for gin then they could do no harm to whisky.

I was surprised at first and then moved, when passing a roadside cross on the Continent, she would say, 'Poor Jesus Christ', and even shed a tear. She never talked about religion, yet she was a woman of faith. She had a simple belief in God, which was beyond question, whilst I questioned the whole business of belief. She was less strong on application, which did not seem to be a problem for her Orthodox faith, whereas I often hid behind my criticism of Christians who did not live out their beliefs in practice. Somehow I came round to the realisation that the sins of others were no excuse for mine. She must have played a part in bringing me to that pragmatic view!

When she bought an expensive designer dress or costume she felt it only fair that I should have a new suit. I would protest about this and point out that I did not need the suit and that, anyway, it made the whole operation, if not twice as costly, at least one and half times. Always to no avail. This accumulation of suits has held me in good stead and I still continue to wear some of them to this day. This happy consequence also goes for Sonja's forethought (then considered to be extravagance!) in buying kitchen utensils, items of décor and bed linen, many of which I am still using and enjoying.

Her involvement in my life has continued well beyond the grave. Even to the extent that I sometimes have the sense of her presence, particularly when I am on the point of doing something wrong and I seem to hear her voice saying, 'Don't do it', and, when I am hesitating to do something right, the same voice says, 'Get on with it'.

Sometime after our visit to Mexico for the International Publishing Association Congress of 1986, Sonja felt unwell. We were living in London and the local GP felt that one of her symptoms, an increase of weight, was due to over-eating and over-drinking. This incensed Sonja as her normally good appetite was much reduced and she had given up alcohol several years earlier.

The GP even handed her the four volumes of the London Telephone Directory and said, 'You are that much too heavy'. The doctor arranged for her to have an X-ray check on her gall bladder to see if there was any recurrence of an earlier problem. The result was negative. However she complained to me of feeling a sharp internal pain when the x-rays were taken. At the time I dismissed this as being imaginary or irrelevant, due to her dislike of technical devices.

When we moved to France two years later, she continued to be swollen, felt increasingly uncomfortable and was quickly tired. We went to a local GP in Le Touquet and he took things more seriously than his British counterpart. He arranged for her to have a series of tests over a period of days as an in-patient at the local clinic. I had always found British doctors very resistant to allowing the patient to have a thorough general check-up. I once asked a doctor about this and he said, 'I don't recommend it. I would never have one myself. I don't want to know if anything is seriously wrong with me. I just want to drop down dead when the time comes.'

After the tests the head of the clinic called me to his office and told me that she was in an advanced stage of Viral Hepatitis B, which she had undoubtedly contracted on our visit to Mexico where it is endemic, and due to the lack of an earlier diagnosis it had so badly affected her liver that no surgery or treatment could bring a cure. He said that with pharmaceutical treatment she might live another two years, but there was always the danger that she would not be able to resist other infections and that there was also the possibility of a brain haemorrhage resulting in a coma. I felt considerable resentment against the London medics who had failed to diagnose her soon enough to have undergone a liver transplant.

When we were on a trip to Paris in the spring of 1990 I became aware that Sonja's condition was worsening. She was very uncomfortable in the car and when we reached our friend's apartment, she stayed inside for several days instead of taking part in our usual social whirl. Such was my insensitivity that this annoyed me rather than causing me concern: I was always proud to show her off to whoever I was meeting, so that they would experience her wit and intelligence. There is a block in some men's heads beyond which it is hard to penetrate.

Her condition eased when we were back in Le Touquet and in July we drove down to Switzerland to take part in an industrial conference, travelling in three easy stages, via overnight stops at a luxury hotel near Epernay in Champagne, a chateau hotel in Burgundy and a converted mill in the Jura. It was a beautiful, almost dreamlike journey, driving slowly through the French countryside by day and enjoying four-star meals and accommodation in the evenings. On the third day we zoomed up the winding mountain road to Caux, above Montreux, and checked into a room with a fabulous view across the Rhone Valley and Lake Leman. The trip was taking on a honeymoon quality. Perhaps that is what it was. Unknowingly, we were on our final honeymoon.

She had some wonderful talks with friends at the conference and was in great heart, although weaker physically. It was during that time at Caux that my rethinking about the media began to take shape and Sonja challenged me to do something about it. She was dressed to perfection on our departure as we waved goodbye to many new friends, none of whom would see her again.

On the way back, at the Epernay hotel, she took dinner in our room and one of her favourite dishes, a special preparation of calves' brains, was on the menu. She had two helpings and even wanted it again for breakfast. When I protested she said quietly, 'I don't think that I'll have the opportunity again.' I learned later from the manageress of the dress department in Harrods that Sonja had said to her on her last visit that she would not be coming again and to thank the staff for their kindness.

We had a quiet week in Le Touquet, followed by a visit from granddaughter Natalie and her mum for a few days. Sonja did her best to look after them, but it took a lot out of her. There followed ten days when she slept most of the time. Then I had to go to the Cromwell Hospital in London for a minor ear operation.

On the evening before the surgery Fred came to see me. He was wearing a pigtail and asked me what I thought of it. I said, 'Not much' and he therewith unscrewed it from the body of his hair and looked normal again. It was news to me that you could get a pigtail made of your own hair and then be able to wear it or not according to taste and circumstances. Fred and I had a rather uncomfortable exchange and I reprimanded him for not having been to see his mother for a year or more. Then we phoned Sonja in France. She sounded somewhat strange, but we both managed to have some kind of conversation with her for a few minutes. These were the last words that we were to have together.

The next morning I was operated on fairly early. I was still under the influence of the anaesthetic when I had what seemed to be a dream. The concierge in Le Touquet phoned me to say that Sonja had fallen very ill and been taken by ambulance to the local hospital. Then I lapsed into unconsciousness again and was not fully awake until mid afternoon. The dream came back to me and I decided to call the concierge and ask if all was well. She was surprised and said, 'But I rang you this morning and told you that I had found her in a state of collapse and semi-consciousness, had called your GP, who immediately ordered an ambulance. She was taken to the General Hospital in Berck, further down the coast.' Forgetting about my own recovery I was galvanised into action, asking for the resident doctor and phoning my surgeon. I told them that I should leave immediately for France, no matter my own state. They protested, but let me go early the next morning and I was back in Le Touquet later that day.

The concierge told me that, as agreed with me, she had called by the flat just after breakfast. There was no response and she used her master key to enter. Inside Sonja was lying on the floor unconscious. She had obviously had a seizure.

I rushed to my car in the underground garage and drove the 20 miles to the hospital in a state of fear and bewilderment. On arrival I was taken straight to her room where she lay breathing noisily, linked up to equipment and surrounded by tubes. She was in a coma and when I talked to her there was no response.

That is the worst thing in this kind of death. You are not able to communicate with the person whom you have loved and lived with for half a lifetime. You talk softly into her ears and hope that your words are getting through in some way.

No one knows. There is no sign of understanding and no reaction. Perhaps deep inside you are transmitting a sense of love and peace. You hope so. And then you pray to whomever out there might listen to you and comfort your grief. You hope that that lucid and creative mind will be surfacing somewhere into the company of earlier loved ones and welcoming angels.

Will her colonel father be there in his smartest uniform and her mother painting a beautiful picture in a magical setting? Will Uncle Peter, her favourite uncle from the heart of Serbia, be helping her along, his wife having prepared one of her delicious meat *sarmas*? Will her half-sister and her husband who had been Tito's doctor be there to explain what has happened? Will she be able to look into a screen and see me there on earth struggling to come to terms with the greatest loss in my life? Will she help me to stay on track and put into effect the destiny that she had foreseen for me, and that she had challenged me to accept? Or would I take the opportunity to turn my back on all that and live a life centred on a soft and pointless retirement?

The following days were filled with all the practicalities of a death. Finding an undertaker, a tombstone sculptor, obtaining a place in the cemetery from the Town Hall, informing the various authorities (and even now, 15 years later I have not succeeded in having her name removed from all official documents and registries), letting all my friends know of her departure, preparing an item for the local press, weekly and daily.

The most exacting was to satisfy her wish that she would have a Serbian Orthodox ceremony. The nearest Orthodox priest was at the Serbian Church in Paris and I travelled down to meet him. His title is Pope, later confused in press reports with Pape. He became *le Pape orthodoxe de Paris*, doubtless an unexpected promotion. I had a good talk with him, telling him some of Sonja's story and he willingly agreed to come to Le Touquet to conduct the Orthodox ceremonies at the Catholic Church and at the graveside. At a well-attended service his chanting and delivery were much appreciated but, alas, being in Serbian, not understood, with two exceptions, a Serbian hotelkeeper and a Serbian dentist, both of whom had married Frenchwomen and lived locally.

I was particularly moved by the presence of my publishing friends from Holland and Britain. The tomb's surroundings in the cemetery were covered with flowers and the weather was kindly. It was a double grave and Sonja was lowered into the bottom place and the top left for me to join her at some later date (my credit card insurance covers bringing me to that final resting place from wherever I pass away in the world). My recollections of these events are not very clear. My mind and heart were elsewhere trying to be with Sonja wherever she was going. It was as though I was partly anaesthetised from the proceedings and the difficulty of grasping that she was gone forever. All human contact had ended with a person of extraordinary dynamism and perception. She had given me a life without a dull moment.

From the cemetery those who had come from afar came with me to our apartment for what the Scots call a 'wake' – a drink, a snack and an exchange of recollections. By late afternoon all my friends had left for home and I was alone. Alone in a more profound sense than I had known before. Fortunately the day's events had been exacting and I flopped down on my bed, fully dressed, into a deep sleep.

In the days that followed there was the painful duty of informing those friends and relatives that I had not been able to contact sooner, often with a sense of unbelief and many times in tears. Later came 50 or more letters of understanding and comfort. An often-recurring theme was appreciation of her direct speaking and fearless confrontations. During those weeks I felt that I might soon be joining her. Gradually I came to terms with her passing and began to focus my mind and actions on what I felt called to do to help to bring a new purpose to the media.

The Next Generation

When I looked at the lives of colleagues and senior business professionals in my last years as the head of a company, the extent of family breakdown and disappointment in the behaviour and instability of their children was widespread. The managing partner of one of the professional firms with whom we dealt told me that he was the only partner of ten who had a stable family life. The others were either divorced or separated from their wives. When I visited the USA I had the impression that divorce among my business friends was endemic, all the more surprising to me as most of them professed a religious belief.

How had my behaviour affected my son and in its turn how did his behaviour affect his daughter? I was devoted to earning money and furthering my career and had very little time to spend with Fred. Even now I can count on the fingers of one hand the occasions when I took him out to a show or on an interesting event. Perhaps Sonja tried too hard to keep him from getting under my feet and we rarely ate meals together at home except during the weekends or on holidays, and the latter were infrequent. And what is the effect on a child of a noisy and accusing row between parents?

Fortunately I never lost communication with Fred and in later life he always assured me that my shortcomings had not damaged his life and that he had been more aware of my good points. His daughter Natalie's life began to break up. She went to a school that catered for children with gifts for the performing arts, which might mean that their mothers thought that they had! Of course there was some genuine talent. Natalie wanted to become a dancer and actress and I would have been happy to see her succeed. I certainly dreamed of boasting that my granddaughter was the star in the latest musical! Natalie was steadily losing her motivation. So when the day came to sit her A-Levels, which she needed to get a university place, she just walked out of the exam room without answering the questions. When I asked her why, she said that she had got completely fed up with being educated since the age of five.

For two or three years I did not see much of her. She was earning money as a hat-check girl or a waitress or any odd job that came her way. She also decided to stop living with her mother and to move in with her father. He made little attempt to discipline her and eventually they were estranged from one another for several years. She had made some friends from well-off families of school days and more or less camped out with them in their homes or flats. During that time she took to drugs and vodka. When later I asked her why vodka, she said that it was because their parents could not smell it.

I never lost faith in her, and I knew that she had the same spark and spirit as her grandmother, and from time to time we used to meet and I would take her out to dinner when I visited London. It was at that time that I had begun to find a new purpose and worthwhile motivation in my own life. This got through to her. I realise now that I had broken the real generation gap, which is that of hypocrisy. When I was genuine, she responded. She knew that I believed in her and that she could trust me. She was completely dejected, had got very thin and was losing her good looks, and all I could do was to listen and be there.

A few months later she turned to me and said – she was about 20 at the time – 'Grandpa, I have two needs in my life.' 'What are they?' I asked. Then she went on, 'I need a spiritual basis and a life purpose and I have neither. How do I get them?' What a question for a grandparent!

I had heard of a leadership-training course in Australia run by Initiatives of Change (the new name for what was formerly called MRA). If she would go, it would lift her right out of London and the company of her dubious friends and, hopefully, give her another chance. She said that she would go, and I was able to persuade her father to pay for the airfare and her stay on the course and even to stay on for longer if she wanted to.

The result was somewhere between remarkable and miraculous. Natalie began to find her spiritual base and her life purpose. She decided to quit dancing and acting because it was just for her own glorification and that she would become a social worker, because it would be directed to helping others. She became completely free of her addiction to drugs and alcohol and her looks and health returned. She worked with others to bring moral and spiritual renewal to people of her generation and helped with a centre for rejected aborigine women in Melbourne. Then she took part in a training activity for the youth of Novosibirsk, the capital of Siberia.

More recently she fell in love with a fine young Australian, Jabez Phillpot, and she asked me to give her away at their marriage. I just made it to the wedding having been in hospital for a hip operation and then an infection for more than two months. The doctors and nurses were determined to get me well for the event and I was ready with a week to spare.

Her wedding was a joyous occasion. I was still a bit shaky on my feet and as I walked her down to the ceremonial point it was a question of who was supporting who! However, we made it in the beautiful surroundings of an elegant garden with an awning, where the priest, the bride and the bridegroom stood. The priest had blessed the ground for the wedding and I asked him if that was provisional, but he said that it was now blessed forever. I was impressed by the commitment that the young couple made – they had written it themselves.

They said:

> *Will you Natalie/Jabez take my hand and explore with me the limitless wonders of this world? .... I will.*

> *Will you promise to share with me your own discoveries and new perspectives in life? .... I will.*

> *Will you dare to dream dreams not yet dreamt with me, finding constant reward and challenge, as we pursue the ongoing adventure of learning who we are as changing people and where we want to go? .... I will.*

> *Will you draw on the strength that comes with true love and content yourself with both the horizons ahead of us and the pathways at our feet? .... I will.*

> *Do you believe in a life centred on the trust of God Almighty? .... I do.*

> *Do you believe in the promise of love? .... I do.*

> *Then I Jabez/Natalie offer to you Natalie/Jabez, strong in my belief, and confident in the lasting power of our love, give myself to you as your husband/wife forever and a day.*

I have just read that more than 40 per cent of births in Britain during 2004 were out of wedlock. Most of them are to single mothers alone, although some have a partner. Does this work? For the two people involved and particularly for the offspring? The young have a right to their own lives but the rest of us have a responsibility to help them. I am convinced that the physical relationship between a man and a woman is best in the context of a marriage. This seems to be the conclusion of thousands of years of life on earth and of the faiths and structures which have developed.

But we have a great tendency to want to bang our heads against the wall to see if it hurts and to learn by our own experience, even if that is painful. My son always said that my advice was good, but that he wanted to check it out his own way and to learn for himself. It is still my view that you don't have to put your hand in a flame to know that you will get burned, when there are plenty of wiser people to tell you that that is so. In any event I am glad that Natalie and Jabez have chosen the route of holy matrimony and I wish them much happiness in loving one another and in helping others.

My Grandmother, my memory, my often forgotten
Written by Natalie Porter, June 1998

My Grandmother, my memory, my often forgotten
My memory of you often fades through carelessness
   and neglect,
Forgive me please for this confession,
And guide my thoughts to you.

Too young to appreciate your culture,
Too naïve to really understand you,
Time ran out against the clock of life and death and love.

I hear stories of your grandness,
Your real love for life.
How I wish I had more time with you,
We could have been the best of friends.

I remember your roar of laughter,
I remember your warm embrace,
Granny, I remember your aura,
You were a lady to be admired.

Granny, you were extravagant,
A trait I think I have gained,
Your love for the exquisite was apparent in your dress.

But behind the larger than life exterior
We must never forget
That deep inside was a woman who had experienced
her fair share of pain.

Your memories became your survival,
Memories you never, never forgot,
Things that people saw as your funny quirks,
Were remainders of your pain.

I see myself in your memories,
A replica of you I have become,
A fighter for survival,
A real heart and soul.

You see I have not forgotten you,
Your memory is still quite clear,
How could I ever forget such a lady as you?

III

Destiny

If not Me, Who?

It is unlikely that any change of direction in human behaviour and purpose takes place just for one reason alone. Even before a change occurs, there are elements at work that provoke it. It is the consequence of a number of factors. And if the change is to be in a creative direction, it needs to have an inner source of inspiration.

In my case there were at least two triggers of change that were decisive. I had also been thinking a fair amount about the state of society and of the role of my world, the media, in affecting it.

The first trigger was reading in *The Financial Times* that the communications industry, including the mass media, had become the largest industry in the world. That led me to ask myself if we were also the most responsible. I felt the answer was a definite NO. Where did I stand as the chief executive of a publishing group, on the issue of responsibility?

I realised that I had never asked myself the question, nor been asked by peers and superiors, 'What is the effect of your products for good or ill on the people who read, listen to and watch them?' If we did something which had a good social effect I was happy to take some praise, but if it had a bad effect I washed my hands of it, saying that those problems were a matter for politicians, religious leaders and sociologists, but not for me. I had freedom to publish. There was freedom of information and the consequences were not my affair.

I thought this through a little further and realised that media people were not like the manufacturers of soap or chocolate. We had a product that affected the lives and hopes and fears of millions of people. We should be ready to stand up and accept responsibility for its effects.

Until that time my business motivations had been primarily to make money and to become important, both for my company and myself. I am not saying that these are necessarily bad motivations, but they lacked the element of responsibility. How to evaluate responsibility? I came to the conclusion that the best guide was the human conscience, that remarkable piece of high technology that is inside us, albeit often covered over with the compromises of a lifetime. It enables us to know what is right or wrong, what is honest or false, what is just or unjust, and the right moral course to take in any situation. I decided that obedience to my conscience would be the future basis for my business and private life.

There were other factors at work. We had just experienced the euphoria of the end of the Cold War and many of us thought that now we had it made for democracy, the free market and the rule of law. This was not to be and we experienced the cold shower of the reality of human greed and ambition. There was the Gulf War and its consequences. Millions were still dying of starvation in Africa and elsewhere. Violence was increasing in the great cities of the West. Poverty and unemployment were seemingly insoluble problems. And ethnic conflict was straddling the globe. The UN noted more than 1,000 flashpoints where ethnic clash was actual or potential. And this was close to home for me, as my wife was Yugoslav and the ghastly tragedy of Bosnia was about to unfold.

Faced with this world scene, what was the role of the media? Had we come from another planet to report on the end of the earth's civilisation and then go back from whence we came? Or were we part of it, with children, grandchildren and loved ones for whom we would like to see a better world? So I felt that an effort had to be made to find a renewed role for the media in building a free and just society.

At that point I decided to talk things over with Sonja, whose instinctive wisdom I had grown to value highly, and to tell her of my new thinking about the media. She listened very carefully and then she looked me in the eyes and said, 'If you are thinking that way, why don't you do something about it?' That was the second trigger that stirred me to action.

I got in touch with several friends in publishing, broadcasting, journalism and advertising and, with some hesitation, told them about my new awareness. I say hesitation, because I was very sensitive to what people thought about me and I did not wish to be laughed at or ignored. But four of my friends responded and it turned out that they had also been thinking about the media's role.

We decided to act with the intention of building up a worldwide network of men and women in the media who believed in ethical values and applied them in their lives, and so would naturally impact their companies and audiences. We called it the International Communications Forum (ICF) because it would be international, would include all communications sectors and would be a genuine forum, not just another organisation. It would be a conscience-to-conscience activity.

Our first move was to hold a conference at the Initiatives of Change centre at Caux in Switzerland, because of its beautiful location and because of the warm welcome given by the organisers. Since then we have held similar conferences in many parts of the world and are now in touch with more than 2,500 media professionals in 114 countries.

I have sometimes been asked the question as to how I would have lived my life if the ICF had not happened. I usually say, 'Playing golf and bridge, going on cruises and chasing comely widows.' Why me? I do not know the answer to that question, but I do know that when I decided to take this road I experienced a sense of inner compulsion that has never left me. Where does it come from, if not from some superior guiding force in the universe?

I now classify myself as a 'lapsed agnostic' though I did not easily accept the concept of a living God. But each morning I take the decision to cooperate with the forces for good in the world, and I cannot deny that some factor is at work in me that maintains my purpose and commitment. All this in spite of physical knocks like a quadruple heart bypass, a snapped Achilles tendon, a smashed sinus, grommets in both ear drums, cataract operations in both eyes, an artificial hip and a double bacterial infection caught in one of London's best hospitals. These are obstacles to be overcome, not blockages of the road.

If anything has been achieved through me, and I am only one of many, and through the ICF, it must be attributed to this experience of inner compulsion. I believe that this inner compulsion can come to any person who seeks for their destiny to be effective in society, a friend to others, a putter-into-practice of moral values.

The first step was to write to my friend Gordon Graham, recently retired Chief Executive of Butterworths, Britain's leading law publishing firm, and a former Chairman of the Publishers' Association. We were, within a week, the same age, both in infantry divisions during World War II and had worked as journalists in our younger days.

The tenor of my letter was that we had both led fascinating and fruitful lives, but was there still something that we could do as we moved towards a new century to secure the freedom and justice that we had once risked our lives for? Our natural field of activity was the media and it was perhaps there that we could do something effective. His response was that we should meet to talk about it. We did, and he decided to work with me.

At the same time I got in touch with Armand de Malherbe, who headed a major advertising company in France, had been President of the European Advertising Association and Vice-Chairman of the Advertising Tripartite body negotiating with the European Commission. I had worked with him during my time in France and knew him to be a man of integrity and vision.

Another person whom I approached was Graham Turner, who has been described as Britain's leading investigative journalist, and is blessed with a great sense of humour. Additionally, I had a long and encouraging talk on the phone with Rajmohan Gandhi, newspaper editor and grandson of the Mahatma, whom I had got to know in India. We decided to invite people we knew in the press, broadcasting and publishing media to take a few days together to look at where we had got things wrong and how we could get them right.

Two of my fellow initiators were unhappy with the idea of meeting in Caux because of its association with Moral Re-Armament (MRA), about which they had strong reservations. One of them said that if we had that link with MRA it would be a rock behind which many, because of their prejudice, would hide themselves from our challenge. I decided to clear with the Caux people that our conference would have its own agenda and that our participants would not be obliged to take part in the MRA sessions.

This was agreed to with the exception that we would be asked to provide a work team to help with the practical running of the centre. So my colleagues agreed to the location. It would coincide with the Caux Conference for Business and Industry in mid-August. There was a certain hesitation about the work teams, but in any case joining them would be a matter of personal choice. In the event most did join.

We were surprised and impressed that a very learned academic chose to do hard work in the garden, weeding the flowerbeds and tending the vegetable plots. It was also good for my pride when, at the last meeting I asked what had most impressed them during the conference, the most senior person said, 'The leader of the vegetable preparation team', a highly original Swiss lady. That first conference brought together 48 participants from 14 countries and 17 media sectors.

On a warm day in August 1991 I picked up my principal co-worker, Hugh Nowell, Chairman of Grosvenor Productions, at the port of Boulogne. With him was Terry Goldsmith, for many years Editorial Director of Blandford Press, a London publishing company. Terry was already beginning to suffer from an illness that would cost him his life in the following year but he threw himself vigorously into the task with us. He gave us the penetrating thought that 'all media is a one-to-one relationship. For good or ill, and even in mass communication, we are addressing one soul at a time.'

I was still fairly well-off at the time, so I had booked us en route to Switzerland at two four-star country hotels with me picking up the bills. I jokingly said that I wanted my colleagues to get used to the life-style of the media magnates whom we would have to convince of our ideas! I doubt if they took me seriously, but in my mind there was an element of truth in it, because I knew that we would have to reach some of the top people in our industry. In fact we were aiming for men and women at all levels, from the young reporter to the multinational owner.

On the third day we drove along the scenic Swiss motorway overlooking Lake Leman, skirted through the suburbs of fashionable Montreux, climbed the zigzagging mountain road to Caux and pulled up outside the main entrance of Mountain House. The conference centre, which had been a hotel at the beginning of the 20th century, had welcomed the royal families and aristocracy of Europe. During World War II it had housed refugees, but in peacetime was bought and refurbished by Swiss people to become a centre for reconciliation.

The next day our participants arrived and located our conference room. That evening an amusing thing happened at a briefing meeting for the participants from the different groups taking part, some four hundred in all. At its end everyone was asked to go to the meeting rooms of the subject of their choice, and the chairman gave the impression that all those concerned about the media could take part in the ICF event.

Consequently more than a 100 people crowded into our room, many standing at the back and others sitting on the window ledges, as well as occupying all the chairs and tables intended for our participants. We managed to cope that evening, but the next day those who were not working in the media were asked to join other groups. But it did show us what a keen interest there was among the people present in the role and influence of the media.

Our sessions went well, with Gordon Graham leading the first day on 'Freedom and Responsibility'. Graham Turner spoke on the second day reminding us forcefully of the need for journalists to apply in their own lives the standards they wanted to see in their nations. 'If we are blowing the whistle on others, let us make sure our own whistles are clean,' was the way he put it.

Armand de Malherbe led the third day's sessions on moral issues in advertising and television. He said that Europe's TV transmitters would soon be beaming out 500,000 hours of programmes annually and that producers and advertisers needed to think hard what effect they would have on the behaviour and morale of their audiences.

There were no dull moments during the working sessions and strong friendships were formed which have stood the test of time, linking professionals from different backgrounds of race, faith, social origin and media experience. This multicultural, multi-faith, harmonious mix has become a continuing feature of the ICF.

Part of the statement of purpose issued by the conference read, 'The communications industry is one of the world's most powerful influences in creating attitudes and affecting the way people live. The aim of the Forum is to promote the ethical and spiritual values which underpin democracy: honesty, unselfishness, the search for truth and the primacy of the individual conscience. All who take part in it are ready to face whatever changes this implies in their personal and professional lives.'

How the ICF works

I never felt that the ICF should become a permanent activity and I hoped that it would not become an organisation. I perceived its purpose as changing the direction of the media, and then disappearing into the sunset. Of course the question arose as to how long it would take to achieve such an objective. At the beginning of the nineties I was aiming at the year 2000 and ten years still felt a long time. I had written to Gordon Graham saying that I thought that our wartime generation had not finished its task and that we should devote the last decade of the 20th century to that end.

When I spoke of that time-frame to a brilliant young executive with the mighty Bertelsmann media group he looked at me with disbelief and said that we should not give it a short-term existence, but establish it as a permanent challenge to this and future generations. It is sure that, as we have developed, the pressure to set up a structure becomes more pressing.

By 2004 we had all the titles – President, Executive Director, six Vice-Presidents, Area and Chapter Representatives, a not-for-profit limited company with a board of directors, and more to come as we seek tax exemptions for contributions and the legal right to own assets. To today's average executive, this situation is normal and he feels quite comfortable in it, as indeed should I, as I have lived for decades in such a context. But I am not really at ease, although I accept it as necessary, whilst trying to keep its straightjacket as loose as possible. Many think that we should have a formal membership and it is important that the people involved have a sense of belonging. But we are not primarily enlisting supporters, welcome though they might be, but trying to change people's mindset and quality of behaviour.

If there is one thing that is widely detested by the public it is hypocrisy, and they sense a lot of it in politics and the media. Ordinary men and women do not present themselves as models of good behaviour, but they have a very good nose for those who do, and those who, behind the façade, are self-seeking and deceitful.

We decided that our main means of taking action would be through meetings and conferences, where media professionals could frankly address the questions of, 'Where have we got it wrong?' and 'How can we get it right?' We would raise the issues with our friends and in our workplaces. I also decided to take a number of journeys to meet colleagues in other lands. There was a time when I was travelling away from home for up to half of the year.

I have slept in more beds than I care to think of and eaten more kinds of meals than I knew existed. It is a great blessing to sleep well and to enjoy everything that is edible! I enjoy heat, perhaps due to working for four years in India where I adapted to 45° to 50°C temperatures without too much trouble. But I do not like the cold and in some icy rooms I was obliged to put jerseys and a heavy dressing gown around me to get to sleep.

From the beginning my closest working colleague was Hugh Nowell, who ran our London office, supervised the conferences and kept an eagle eye on our finances. His wife Carolyn who is a Californian, but also a fully-adopted Englishwoman, looked after the computerised mailing list which grew under her care. She was an ace at keeping the list clean, an essential but often neglected task.

But the Nowells were more than reliable practical performers; they were great human beings who deeply cared for others. For me as a widower they gave me a lifeline of support and friendship and were not afraid to offer me correction when I started to go down wrong paths or behaved in my old hard managing-director fashion.

I had often met Hugh during my business life at the annual Frankfurt Book Fair, the major event of the international publishing industry. His father had been a leader of Britain's tanning industry and Hugh achieved an honours degree in chemistry at Oxford with a view to following him in the company. Instead he had been drawn to the work of MRA, and had decided to work full-time in its ranks.

After many years travelling with their teams in Asia, America and Europe, he returned to London and took on their book and magazine publishing work. He had begun to hand over this job to a younger colleague at the time the ICF began to appear and felt that he would join me to help get it off the ground and then to keep it flying. This was a great blessing. I do not see how the Forum could have progressed in the way that it has without him and I am deeply grateful for his commitment.

Of the 48 people who took part in our first conference, it is interesting to know that 44 have stuck with us and of the four who didn't, two have died and are, I imagine, still backing us up from a heavenly location! So this original group were the base of people from which the whole operation was developed. It is essentially a person-based activity. Its progress depends on the sincerity and application of those involved.

We have held further conferences in Australia, South Africa, the USA, Canada, Russia, Poland, the Czech Republic, Hungary, Bosnia, France, England, India, Sri Lanka, Ireland, Jamaica, and Scotland. And we are welcomed each summer at the Caux centre. Each conference has been a self-financing undertaking, largely through local contributions and sponsorships. We have enjoyed fascinating locations – a hotel-boat moored on the Volga; a Jesuit hostel in the hills outside Budapest; the forest-surrounded training centre of the Polish

Journalists Union; the City Hall of Pardubice, the Czech Republic's horseracing town; the London *Financial Times* new conference facility; an hotel facing the celebrated Bondi Beach near Sydney; an Indian senator's New Delhi home; the Renaissance Hotel in Denver at the foot of the Rocky Mountains; the Cantigny estate outside Chicago of the McCormick Tribune Foundation; the Palais de l'Europe of the Le Touquet French resort town.

In addition I have travelled to many cities to meet people, to address students at journalism schools and to speak at media association congresses. These journeys covered the USA and Canada from coast to coast, all the capitals of the Australian States, the long train trip from Johannesburg to Cape Town, major cities in India and distant Nagaland, the Lebanon, Jamaica and other Caribbean islands and almost every capital of Europe.

In 1998 I was invited to speak at the annual convention of the American Society of Professional Journalists, a prestigious body of the USA media, when it was held in Los Angeles. On that trip I experienced two views of the public about their media. At Washington Airport, the official checking my entry visa asked me why I was visiting the States. I said that I had been invited to speak at Schools of Journalism and Media conferences. 'What are you going to tell them?' was his next question. 'I'm going to talk about the responsibility of the media for their effect on society,' I replied. He looked at me hard, saying, 'Thank God that someone is doing that. I tremble every time I see my daughters watching our television.' He stamped the visa into my passport with great vigour and wished me the best of luck.

The second incident was when I slipped out of the convention hotel to a small local post office to buy stamps. A rather elderly lady was serving me and, noticing my English accent, asked me why was I in Los Angeles. I said that I was talking at the SPJ convention on the need for the press to clean up their own act and to work for a better society. Then she said, 'I am so grateful that someone is doing that and I would like to thank you for myself and on behalf of my grandchildren.'

These two anecdotes, as well as solid quantitative research, show that the American people look for higher standards in their media. I do not believe that our public consists of violence-loving, sex-mad, moronic idiots, but of hardworking, family-loving, reasonable people, who would like to see a free and just society.

A number of influential people became strong supporters of the ICF's action. They included Senator Jara Moserova of the Czech Republic, who was for a time Vice-President of the Senate and for two years President of the General Conference of UNESCO; Judge David Edward, CVO, British Member of the European High Court of Justice in Luxembourg; Roger Parkinson, Chairman of Canada's leading paper, the *Globe and Mail*, and a President of the World Association of Newspapers; Cornelio Sommaruga, former President of the International Red Cross; Olivier Giscard d'Estaing, Vice President of the European Movement and Chairman of the INSEAD Business School; Sir Howard Cooke, Governor General of Jamaica; John Fairfax, Chairman of Marinya Media and the Rural Press, Australian publishing groups; Toshiaki Ogasawara, President of *The Japan Times*; several members of the British House of Lords; Allan Griffith, special advisor on foreign affairs to Australian Prime Ministers; A R K Mackenzie, former British Ambassador to Tunisia and then at the United Nations; Hans van den Broek who became Foreign Minister of the European Union; Jean-Loup Dherse of the World Bank; David Flint, Chairman of the Australian Broadcasting Commission; and Dr Zaki Badawi, Chairman of the Imams and Mosques Council of Great Britain.

We were especially concerned to meet and dialogue with the younger generation of journalists and broadcasters and were invited to speak to the students and staff at Schools of Journalism and of Media Studies in Ottawa, Toronto, Miami, Harvard, New Delhi, Brisbane, Aberdeen, Glasgow, Edinburgh, Chennai (Madras), Stellenbosch and Cape Town. I was always struck by the enthusiasm with which they greeted our talks based on practical examples of applying ethical values in hard situations.

Martyn Lewis, for many years a popular TV news presenter with the BBC, joined our ranks. Some years earlier he had made a study of the nature of BBC Home News broadcasts and found that they overwhelmingly reported what was going wrong in the world and very sparingly informed their viewers of what was going right. He felt that this was a gross imbalance, perhaps even a misinformation, creating a depressed, sceptical attitude in the public.

Against the wishes of his seniors in the BBC, despite a threat of dismissal, he decided to go public on his findings and to mount a campaign for better balance. A great number of viewers told the BBC that they agreed with him and that lifted the danger of his being fired. But he was also misrepresented by some people in the media who accused him of trying to promote a good-news-only policy. He had a hard battle to refute this, but continued his campaign for balance, in which he was fully supported by the ICF. A video was made of one of his talks and we were able to show this on many occasions.

To strengthen our impact on media education we held a special conference at Caux chaired by Torben Krogh, a Copenhagen daily editor, Chairman of the Danish School of Journalism at Aarhus and recently President of the General Conference of UNESCO. He also became one of the Forum's Vice- Presidents. Media professors and lecturers attended from the USA, South Africa, Jamaica, Ireland, Russia, Poland and the UK. The report was distributed to several hundred media schools across the world.

It is a sign of progress in any reformist venture to be attacked, so I am somewhat surprised that the ICF and I have not come in for more stick. Perhaps the main hostility has shown itself in efforts to diminish its importance. One senior person called us 'a bunch of harmless protestant idealists'. That was hard to take: our main leadership consists of two Roman Catholics, one Hindu, two humanists, two agnostics, one Orthodox, one Episcopalian and one non-conformist. Our Catholic President commented that he was honoured to be associated with 'Protestant idealists'!

Some hostility came because I claimed to have a sense of inner compulsion, which 'might' have been implanted by a superior source of wisdom. Therefore I was a sort of 'fundamentalist' and could be lumped along with all those extremists who seemed to have always been, and still are, fomenters of conflict and division in the world. Personally I don't know how anyone achieves anything of significance for human progress without a strong inner conviction to bring it about. I do not think that civilisation is maintained or advanced by rudderless, indifferent, unmotivated individuals.

I am inclined to feel that the low level of opposition is because it is very difficult to attack genuinely expressed convictions held by reasonable men and women. The change of direction and of behaviour that I have undergone in my own life is not an opinion, it is a fact.

I know that I do not always live up to the ideal, but I am trying hard and, when I fail, I resume the contest and return to the good road. Of course others can disagree or not wish to be involved and that is fair enough. Harder to sympathise with are the reactions, 'I do not wish to be honest, therefore I will attack honesty and those who are practising it.'

One publishing friend said to me: 'But I believe in being broad-minded.' I asked him what he meant by being broad-minded and he replied, 'Well, I suppose I mean that everything I do wrong is right within reason!' As the French say, 'Yes, that is a point of view!' But probably not a sustainable development!

At Sarajevo in 2000 Bernard Margueritte, a senior French

journalist, told me that he was ready to take over the active leadership of the ICF, and in recent years he has done that with imagination and panache. We still try to work as a pair of in-line horses pulling a stagecoach or co-drivers of a high-speed train.

Bernard is a great colleague, who is also a good friend. The French/English relationship is sometimes difficult. But this is no reason not to work together for great enterprises. Because a task is difficult is not a reason not to undertake it. And what relationship does not have its highs and lows? We both have a sense of humour that enjoys the differences and enhances the teamwork.

It has taken me some years to explain to Bernard the differences between assurance, ensurance and insurance and to convince him that no things in English have a gender. Conversely I must cause him linguistic pain when I hopelessly mix up the male and female identification of French nouns and get wrong the *tu* and *vous*, thee and you, relationship with people. The blessings of English are its neutral gender and its single you. Blessings of French are its clarity of expression, its logic and its interjections such as *Et alors!* (So what then?)

Bernard is a polyglot, speaking Polish, English, German and French, high Sorbonne and low Normand. He has the blessing of the total support of his family in spearheading the Forum, with his enchanting wife Joanna, a professor of architecture at Warsaw University, his son Eryk, a pilot with Air France; and last, but decidedly not least, his fearless and highly intelligent daughter, Joanna II, who is showing great promise as a writer, having been editor of her school magazine and written articles and news releases at our conferences.

I am not forgetting Bernard's considerable working experience, first as a journalist for ten years with *Le Monde*, then for ten years with *Le Figaro*, and then for periods with French television and radio. Interspersed with that he was a Research Fellow at Harvard, a visiting professor at the University of

South Carolina, with fellowships at Harvard's Kennedy School and their Russian Research Center.

For most of the time he was located in Warsaw and Vienna and is one of France's outstanding East European foreign correspondents. He ran into trouble with *Le Figaro* when, at the height of the Communist period, he was reporting the Communist leadership as well as the opposition to them. His editor said that their readers were anti-Communist and did not want to read about what Marxist leaders were saying in East Europe. Bernard felt that his job was to report what all sides were saying and doing, regardless of his or his paper's opinions. The editor was adamant and they parted ways.

He was always grateful for the grounding in journalism that he received from Hubert Beuve-Méry, the legendary founder of *Le Monde* after World War II. As a young journalist, rather full of himself, and proud to be working for an already famous paper, he wrote an article on the Polish situation which was peppered with phrases such as: 'in my opinion', 'I think that', 'the Poles should', 'it seems to me' and so on.

Most reports and articles were seen by Beuve-Méry before going to press and when he read Bernard's piece he called for him. Bernard entered the large office where he was seated at what seemed like a long distance from the door, and in considerable apprehension stumbled towards the great man, who was waving Bernard's article in the air and saying, 'What's this? You think this and you think that. What Bernard Margueritte thinks is not of the slightest interest to the readers. Your job is to report the facts and to include the opinions of the parties concerned, but certainly not yours. Then the readers can form their own views.'

A few months later Bernard was asked to write one of the editorials and his senior took him to Beuve-Méry's office to clear it for publication. Bernard went in by himself and B-M read his efforts, then he gave a grunt, and waved Bernard out without saying a word. His editor, waiting nervously outside the door, asked him what happened. 'Nothing,' said Bernard. 'He just went urghh.' 'Oh, great,' said his editor, 'that means that he liked it.'

Do Bernard and I always see eye to eye? Or do we sometimes have disagreements? It is more likely that we have misunderstandings due to the finesse of language or misinterpretation of particular issues owing to our different knowledge backgrounds. How can it be otherwise in the interplay between human beings? What is never in question is our common motivation to see our media world become a positive force in the life of our times.

Following one contretemps some of my friends thought that a solution could only be brought about by prayer, in order to restore understanding between both of us. From previous experience, I had to be close to death or financial disaster to turn to prayer, but I told my colleagues to go ahead. Something must have happened, because the next morning Bernard came over to me at breakfast and humbly restored our relationship.

I met Robin Williamson when I was Deputy Chairman of Publishers Databases Ltd and he applied for the job of Director. Later on, for a short time I was Deputy Chairman of a CD Rom firm of which he was Managing Director. I left when it changed ownership, but Robin continued and made a great success of the company's development.

Shortly after my retirement, when I was living in France, I invited him to one of the early ICF's conferences, which was sponsored by the Member of Parliament and Mayor of Le Touquet, Léonce Deprez. Robin came and after listening carefully throughout the conference got to his feet in the last session and thanked me for the lead that I had given and said that he would commit his own life to forwarding the Forum's ideas.

Nearly ten years later, when he heard that Hugh Nowell wanted to retire from his administrative functions with the ICF in London, he volunteered to take over from him. He has since devoted his considerable abilities to that task as our

Executive Director, including management of the mailing list and updating our Internet website. Robin is a man of faith and foresight and is proving to be a worthy right-hand man for Bernard. Robin's charming wife, Priscilla, has entertained us at her home in Sussex on several occasions.

Robert Webb is an American Southerner, a graduate of the Missouri School of Journalism, which claims to be the world's oldest (certainly true for North America), a reporter with city dailies, was head of the Washington Bureau of the *Cincinnati Enquirer* and later an editorial committee member, and is now the Forum's Vice-President for the Americas. Bob is a much-loved and respected figure in the US print media scene.

From being a journalist who was always looking for the weaknesses and misdeeds of the politicians and civic and business leaders about whom he was reporting, he had decided to write in a way that could help and inspire those men and women to serve their communities honestly and effectively. When he heard about the ICF he was naturally drawn to it and has headed up its activities in his country ever since.

From the very beginning of the ICF, Jean-Jacques Odier, from Geneva, took responsibility for our development in the French-speaking world. He was a member of a two-centuries-old Swiss banking family and had turned down a career in the firm to work full-time with MRA, particularly with the trade unions and in industrial relations. His play on the life of Jean Jaurès, the great socialist leader, won a Geneva prize of the year, and he edited the Paris-based magazine, *Changer*.

Le Touquet has turned out to be a good location for my work with the Forum. I can get to London from Calais by Eurostar in one hour twenty minutes, shortly to be reduced to one hour, when the new fast track on the English side is completed. I can reach Paris in just over one hour and Brussels in forty minutes. I can comfortably drive to Paris in two and a half hours or to Caux in one and a half days with an overnight stop, and I can be in Kent by car within an hour. When the

World Association of Newspapers Congress was in Bruges I drove there in less than two hours. Beauvais Airport, from which the low-cost airlines fly to many European locations, is about one and a half hours by car.

* * * * * * *

One of the most remarkable aspects of the Forum has been its financing. After more than 14 years of activities across all the continents, there are no unpaid bills, but nor is there any reserve in the coffers for future developments and planned projects. But I am convinced that they will take place.

Being of North Lancashire origin I am reminded of an expression from my home county: 'Put your money where your mouth is.' When the Forum was launched in 1991 I was reasonably well off with six-figure life savings and an adequate, if not over-generous, clutch of pensions. After ten years of covering my own costs and meeting Forum shortfalls, my savings are reduced to zero and I am allocating half of my pension income to Forum activities.

To date the ICF has never paid a speaker's fee nor a salary. In most cases people active with it have covered their own travel and accommodation costs, with the exception of those coming from former Communist countries and the developing world, where good pay and hard currency have been in short supply. The financing of each conference has been undertaken separately and largely at the responsibility of the country of its location. At least 24 conferences have been held and in most cases there were also preparation visits of experienced people from other parts of the world, the expenses of which needed to be covered. I suppose that the single major cost today is airfares for those setting up and taking part, followed closely by hotel bills and conference facilities. Printing and sending out invitations and then reports cost a lot too.

We are now approaching the undertaking of special projects

in the fields of research, journalists' exchanges, video production, a go-anywhere values-workshop, e-mail journals, website maintenance and a prize for young journalists. All these are taking us into the area of what is blithely described as 'real' money. It is only with major donations from foundations, trusts, companies and wealthy individuals that we shall be able to tackle these enterprises.

Sponsorship has been a major factor in conference financing. Companies and associations have provided meals, receptions, printing costs, sight-seeing tours for foreign participants, transport, simultaneous translation facilities, local publicity, electronic and audio recording of the proceedings and even, in one case, some free rounds of golf.

Contributions have come from many sources, but mainly from media activities and concerned individuals. One consultant gave a major fee resulting from a successful acquisition deal. Two multinational publishing firms have given reasonable sums and we need many more to follow – after all we are trying to persuade them not to saw off the branch on which they are sitting.

At a public meeting in a North of England town one of the speakers happened to mention the work of the ICF and that it needed supporting. An individual approached him afterwards and asked for our address. A few days later he sent in a cheque for £500 with a note saying that, although he was retired, he was so dismayed by what he was reading in the press and seeing on the television that he wanted to help our cause.

We do make regular annual appeals to most of the names on our ever-growing mailing list, although, as more than half of them are from poorer countries, this is not a great source of funds. Nevertheless there are some people who give regularly. We are now aiming to build up a group of benefactors who will undertake to give for a minimum of three years, and intend to develop an 'associate' concept for companies and associations.

Béla Hatvany, a successful CD Rom publisher of Hungarian

origin, took part in our meetings and offered to underwrite the travel and other costs and the loss of earnings of a successor to myself as the active President. This coincided exactly with Bernard Margueritte telling me that he was ready to take on this role and Béla's offer enabled us to assure Bernard that financial support would be available for a two-year period.

Bernard has travelled the world – twice to North America, three times to South Africa, twice to the Lebanon, and to Brazil, India, Russia, Portugal, New Zealand, Austria, Belgium, Australia and many times to Britain, France and Switzerland. He has spoken at the annual conferences of major media bodies such as the International Press Institute and the World Association of Newspapers, at Schools of Journalism and business seminars.

On another occasion a man carrying a famous name in the book world telephoned me. It was near the end of the year and he asked me if the Forum would end up solvent on 31 December and, if not, by how much. I told him that we would be short by several thousands of pounds. 'Right,' he said, 'a cheque will be in the post tomorrow for the sum.' And so it was!

Our biggest undertaking to date has been the World Assembly SARAJEVO 2000. It involved the largest budget that we had ever had to face, and in a country with 50 per cent unemployment. So we had to widen the appeal to beyond Sarajevo, although the Cantonal Government financed a reception, Centrotrans provided local transport and Logosoft supplied computer equipment.

We had been promised $5,000 from one source, but at the last minute it was withdrawn and we were in distress. But the Karl Popper Foundation gave $5,000, and other financial help came from the Robert Hahnloser Foundation, the French publisher Media Participations, the Caring Institute of Great Britain and the Swiss Foreign Office. In the end, not only did we clear all costs for the Assembly, print a full-colour maga-zine report of the event, and produce a 13-minute video cassette, but were able to make a contribution to the overhead costs of the London office.

Finally I want to pay tribute to my dear friend, John Rose, a highly competent chartered accountant, who had been a company auditor and my personal consultant and who was a senior partner in a well-established London practice. For 10 years he handled the receipts and payments accounts of the ICF and gave us valued financial advice without charging a penny.

The Pilgrim Road

The future direction of the media may well be decided in the United States of America. They are providing 70 per cent of the world's visual media – film, television and videos. Their major newspapers have a global impact. The tradition of the freedom of the press goes back to the frontier days and is defended tenaciously. But, in spite of the USA's major role on the world scene, the focus of their media seems to have been more on the issues in their own back streets and prairie farms than where humanity is tearing itself apart in distant continents. After all, for the most part they are not selling their papers or directing their advertising to people beyond their own boundaries.

In contrast, and perhaps without the American people realising it, the US media radiate influence in fashions, music, and Hollywood portrayals of daily life, and are powerfully impacting the rest of the world for better or worse.

My own contact with Americans had begun during the war when I served with British units under the US First Army in North Africa and the Fifth Army in Italy. I had nothing but good memories of those times, respecting their courage and admiring their equipment. Later, during my publishing life, I made several business journeys to the USA.

Among the Americans who took part in our first conferences at Caux were Ron Nahser, the head of a Chicago advertising company, and Marie Arana-Ward, a Vice-President of the great publishing house of Simon and Schuster, as well as Bob Webb. During the 1992 Caux event they were taking part in a meeting about the ICF's future activities, when a British journalist turned to Nahser and said, 'Why don't you start something in Chicago?' Ron blinked hard, but since a Mid-Westerner cannot refuse a challenge, he agreed to think about it. The three Americans also invited me to come to the USA and see what interest we could stir up.

Marie was a brilliant book editor and later became book, and for a time education editor of the *Washington Post*. She was of mixed Peruvian and United States stock and inherited the good looks of both peoples. Her husband was a director of a major hotel group. I was fortunate to be asked to stay at their home when I was in Washington, where I was wonderfully looked after, introduced to media people and shown the town.

Bob Webb was my host in Cincinnati, where we met many of his colleagues on his own and the rival paper. One evening Bob took me into an icecream parlour, where he was recognised by a uniformed state serviceman with 21 medals, who said that he read every word of Bob's articles and considered him to be a mainstay of the paper. When I mentioned this to Bob's News Editor the next day, he said, 'Oh yes! Bob has a man like that in every ice-cream parlour in town! It gives a good impression!'

Ron Nahser was my idea of a dynamic American advertising man; he was running a very successful business with a top-notch creative team. In Chicago, he put me up at the prestigious Chicago Club, which boasts a dining table once owned by Samuel Johnson of dictionary fame. For the first time I was in America on Thanksgiving Day and Ron invited me to a magnificent family feast at his home in nearby Evanston, further along Lake Michigan. His wife Mary and three of their four talented and vivacious daughters were present.

Ron and I visited Jack Fuller, editor of the great *Chicago Tribune*, and after telling him about the ideas and work of the Forum he said, 'Well, I don't believe in associations, but I do believe in people and that is the way you seem to be going. I think that your first conference in the USA should be held at the McCormick Tribune Foundation property in the country to the West of Chicago.' He arranged for us to visit Cantigny, as it is called, named after the first French town recaptured by the US Army in the First World War, in which the young Robert McCormick was a major, and who became the famous publisher of the *Tribune* between the two world wars.

At Cantigny we were received by Richard Behrenhausen, its Chief Operating Officer and a recently retired young General of the 1st US Infantry Division. He quickly agreed to provide the facilities for our event and fixed the dates for 30 April to 3 May in 1993, the same year that we were invited to Russia's third city, Nizhny Novgorod. It seemed remarkable, if not miraculous, that the ICF would be landing in two of the most significant nations of the century within a few months of one another.

I returned to America shortly before the Cantigny Conference to find the Nahser family and the advertising agency hard at work preparing for the event, especially two highly competent ladies, Ron's wife Mary, and his company secretary, Florence Agosto. If something needed to happen they could make it happen!

Rome was preparing for the Jubilee Year of 2000 as Bernard Margueritte and I arrived there in May, 1999 for an audience with the Pontiff. There were road works and building sites everywhere – a beautiful city, which would be even more so when completed. At the Pope's Pentecostal Mass, in St Peter's Square with a congregation in excess of 30,000 people, we were placed in a privileged enclosure. Bill Porter at a church service for three hours? Seated just in front of us were 15 rejoicing Nigerian nuns, and beside and behind were the citizens of Rome. We had been supplied with candles and at the end of the communion, given by a host of priests circulating among the throng, these were lit. What a fantastic sight!

Thousands and thousands of lights flickering across the square as night fell. And then an open version of the Popemobile, gleaming white, arrived to take His Holiness on a tour of the whole square, so that everyone could receive his blessings.

Some weeks earlier in Warsaw, Bernard Margueritte was talking with the Papal Nuncio to Poland and telling him about the ICF. The Nuncio said that the Pope should know about this, as he was deeply concerned about the role of the media. When Bernard asked him how this could happen, he said, 'Well, I was a seminarist with John Paul and I am sure that I can persuade him to meet you.' A few weeks later we were summoned to Rome.

Having reached the time of our appointment with the Pope, the process of getting to him was quite elaborate. Firstly, we passed beneath a huge bronze gateway to present our official letter to the colourfully-uniformed Swiss guards, of which there are 270 in all. They were firm and courteous and, once that they were sure of our validity, ushered us through various other checkpoints, across a vast inner courtyard and into the Pope's residential building. There we ascended vast flights of stairs (we only found the lift when coming down) to the top floor where the Pope lives and works. We were met by distinguished figures in dark morning dress who gave us a final clearance and then ushered us into a magnificent hall whose walls were hung with tapestries and murals – a feast of fine art.

After a short wait we were moved through several anterooms while the people shepherding us changed from officials to bishops, who chatted with us and made us feel welcome. We were temporarily bypassed as the Mayor of Moscow, Luzhkov, went through by himself to be followed a few minutes later by a rather nervous wife, dressed in a tight-fitting brand-new, white costume; and then about eight dark-suited, rather apparatchik-looking men with some photographers and TV cameramen.

'Does the Pope know that the Mayor is accused of being a crook?' we asked ourselves. 'Yes,' we were told later. Fortunately, you don't have to be good to meet the Pontiff.

Then the word came that it was our moment and in we went into a large and splendid room with the Pope getting up from behind his old-style, substantial working desk to greet us. He shook me strongly by the hand and Bernard followed by inclining and kissing the Holy Father's ring. We sat down in roomy but sensible chairs with space on the desk to put down our papers. We had been asked to bring documentation about the Forum.

Soon everyone else had left the room and we were alone with His Holiness, who was relaxed and friendly. He was dressed in white robes and cap, with snowy hair peeking out from around it. His complexion was smooth with few lines and he did not wear glasses. I sensed great compassion and understanding in his eyes and he looked straight at us when we talked.

Bernard told him the ICF story in fluent Polish and he listened with close attention, making the occasional comment on points that he felt to be important. He clearly felt that men and women in the media, of all faiths and of goodwill and of no faith should work to maintain and strengthen democracy. Words poured out of Bernard like a river in flood, with passion and strong conviction. And, in the light of the Pope's forthcoming visit to Poland, he hoped that he would challenge the Polish people to rise to the destiny of giving moral leadership to Europe. At that the Pope gave a wry smile.

He and I exchanged a few words about our age, as we were both born in the same year. I told him of the change of direction in my life from being driven by money and success to realising the responsible and inspiring role that we in all media sectors could give to society.

After about 20 minutes one of his bishops opened a door to see if the meeting was ending, but the Pope waved him back and then said to Bernard in Polish, 'They are pushing us,' and we carried on a little longer. On leaving he shook us warmly by the hand and said, 'My blessings for your activity.' His blessing was not just for us, but also for all those taking part in our work. He then gave each of us the bronze medallion celebrating his 20 years as Pope and a beautiful silver and black-beaded rosary. At the lift on the way out we crossed with the Crown Prince of Saudi Arabia, his Deputy Prime Minister and a distinguished retinue dressed in flowing Arab robes and splendid head-dresses. Finally, back through the Swiss guards and out into the bustling animation of St Peter's Square.

We called at the office of Archbishop John Foley, President of the Pontifical Council for Social Communications. He is the cleric responsible for the mass media and all forms of communication. He had met Bernard two or three weeks earlier in Poland and regretted being unable to see us in Rome, as he was in the USA at the time of our visit, but wanted us to leave documentation for his return.

Radio Vatican tracked down Bernard to give an interview on the ICF and our visit to Rome. It lasted for more than 20 minutes and was broadcast on the Polish-language service that evening and twice on the following day. It could have been heard by Polish listeners throughout the world. We visited the Holy See Press Office. We were taken to lunch by Caroline Bouan, who heads the Media International Press Agency bureau (part of the Media Participations Group in Paris), and were joined by Père Vandrisse, *Le Figaro*'s long-standing Vatican correspondent.

Cardinal Paul Poupard, President of the Pontifical Council for Culture, received us in the impressive Palazzo San Carlo and we had a good half-hour exchange with him. He is particularly interested in the ICF's activities with cinema and theatre. A visit to the offices of the Vatican daily, *L'Osservatore Romano*, followed, where we met Father Czeslaw Drazek, editor of the Polish-language magazine issue of the paper.

The Head of the Polish Catholic House in Rome looked after our visit with great care and booked us into the Guest House Pension of the Maestre Pie Filippini Sisters, a well-cared for establishment for the use of pilgrims, and about 15 minutes walk from the Vatican. Our audience with the Pope gave the sisters some excitement and we were warmly introduced to the Mother General of the Order on the occasion of her visit. I was deeply moved two days after returning to France to receive an e-mail from the Sister in charge saying: *Dear Mr Porter... what a pleasure to meet you and hear of the great work of the ICF. Mother General and I have read the literature you left with Sister Nicolina at the Pensione. What a difference your group can make for the world! If there is ever any way we can be of help to you please let me know. Be assured of our prayers for the success of your mission. God bless you. Sister Mary Elizabeth Lloyd, MPF.*

I returned to former Yugoslavia with retired British diplomat, Archie Mackenzie. Sonja and I had got to know him and his wife Ruth when he was British Consul General based in Zagreb. He went on to become Ambassador to Tunisia and his last diplomatic appointment was as British Representative on the Economic and Social Council of the United Nations in New York. We went to Belgrade together to support friends trying to bring sanity and hope to that desperate situation. A cousin of my wife kindly met us at the airport and sacrificed much of his small supply of petrol to accompany us when he could. Otherwise we travelled in absolutely overcrowded trams, one of the few remaining means of transport, which we used frequently in frozen and snowbound conditions.

The British treat intellectuals with much suspicion and little appreciation. Our visit to Belgrade was greeted by one of the papers with the headline, 'Visit of leading British intellectuals'. We devoutly hoped that no one back home would hear about it! We met Milovan Djilas, whom Mackenzie had known before. Djilas was one of the most feared of Tito's early associates. One man told me that during those days Djilas had critically interviewed him with a parabellum pistol aimed across the desk. He had the reputation of being a hard liner. But something happened to him that caused him to reject Communism and to turn towards democratic solutions. He wrote two books, *The New Class* and *Conversations with Stalin*, which earned him several years of imprisonment and house arrest. He received us in his apartment, not too far from the Orthodox Cathedral, where later his grandchildren were baptised. His meetings with Mackenzie and a Norwegian resistance fighter, Leif Hovelsen, had helped to renew his faith in building a better society based on moral values. His son, Alexis, who had graduated at Harvard, turned his back on a comfortable job in the USA and returned to Serbia to help in its reconstruction.

The tragic Bosnian conflict had torn apart the territories and the people. Why did that disaster occur? Many believe that it was due to religion and history. This may be true in part, but I do not think that this was the basic reason. That lay in the ambitions and greed in men's hearts and minds. The small-time politician who wanted to be a cabinet minister, the captain in the army who wanted to be a general, the street trader who wanted to be a big businessman, the frustrated psychiatrist who wanted to be a national figure.

All these selfish aims led many men and some women to exploit the bad memories of ethnic persecution during World War II, the resentments about discrimination by majorities against minorities and bruised vanities. In the end there was the Dayton Agreement, which provided a solution on paper, but not in the hearts of people because many of the fears, suspicions and hatreds remain to this day and it will fall to other generations to resolve them.

In 1998, I returned to Sarajevo with a Polish journalist, Jan Pièklo, who had reported the conflict and also driven a supply lorry. To me it was heart breaking, but to my colleague it was with a sense of relief that he could walk the streets in safety.

The city had endured three years of daily shellfire, destroying the main buildings in the centre, including the National Library with 300,000 books and manuscripts. One could not see a building or a house that had not been hit or pockmarked. The headquarters of the main daily newspaper, *Oslobodenje*, had been completely destroyed above ground. The Central Station, from which I had once taken the train to Dubrovnik, was an empty shell with sheep grazing between the lines.

In 2000 the ICF held there a Media World Assembly called SARAJEVO 2000. It took place in the Holiday Inn, which had housed foreign journalists during the siege. Broken windows had been replaced and facilities had been restored. More than 180 journalists from 21 countries filled the conference room to reflect on the theme of 'The Media – a decisive force in building a free and just society'. Among those taking part were journalists and broadcasters from many nations including India, Russia, Poland, Nigeria, Jamaica, the USA, the Czech Republic, Ireland, Holland, Britain, France and the countries of the former Yugoslavia.

One result was The Sarajevo Commitment (printed in full as an Appendix). Later Jay Rosen, Professor of Journalism at New York University, compared it with the Gettysburg Address and the United Nations Charter of Human Rights calling it 'a document of historical importance'. It has since been translated into 17 languages and gone round the globe. Instead of being yet another conference resolution, it was an individual commitment on the part of the media people present. The first one to sign it was Mehmed Husić, President of the Bosnian Independent Journalists Association. Of 90 present when it was launched, 80 signed it on the spot.

It had been deeply moving to hear Kemal Kurspahić, wartime editor of *Oslobodenje*, tell the story of the shelling and near destruction of their ten-storey building during the siege and of how they had continued to bring out the paper without the loss of one day.

23. IC Forum, Caux, Switzerland, 1992. Anatoli Yaroshevskiy, Moscow TV presenter, seeks reconciliation with the Lithuanian representatives.

24. Cantigny, USA, 1993. *L-r:* Senator Eugene McCarthy, Roger Parkinson, Publisher, *Toronto, Globe & Mail*, Gordon Graham, former President British Publisher's Association in discussion at the McCormick-Tribune Centre

25. Nizhny Novgorod, Russia, 1993. A light moment on the Albatros Hotel Boat, location of the Forum, with Vladimir Suprun, President of the Novosibirsk Business Ethics Association

27. Sarajevo, 2000. Bosnian and Serb students from the Media Plan School of Journalism participate in the conference.

26. Sarajevo, Bosnia-Herzogovina, 1997. Uniforms still on the streets

28. Prague, Czech Republic, 1998. The Senate President (*left*) welcomes Torben Krogh, Chairman, Danish School of Journalism, with Senator Jara Moserova, and Tomas Vrba of the Association of European Journalists.

29. Bondi Beach, Sydney, Australia, 1997. Sir Zelman Cowan, former Governor-General, Dr Jara Moserova, Czech Senator and Rajmohan Gandhi, author and journalist

30. The Vatican, 1999. Pope John Paul II receives me and Bernard Margueritte in his private office.

31. Ireland, 1999. International speakers en route to an IC Forum in Ballina, Co. Mayo

32. Newcastle upon Tyne, UK, 2000. Speakers at a public conference on the role of the Media. *L-r*: Stephen Whittle, Director, Broadcasting Standards Commission, Sir David Bell, Chairman, Financial Times and Lord David Puttnam, Film Director

33. Capetown, South Africa, 2003. Dr Essop Pahad, Minister in the Presidency welcomes international participants including delegates from 17 sub-Saharan countries.

34. Aberdeen, Scotland, 2001. The Lord Provost's Reception at the Town House. *L-r*: Bernard Margueritte, Dr Allan MacDonald, Cllr Len Ironside, Ian Johnson, Robert Gordon University, myself and Martyn Lewis, TV presenter

35. Columbo, Sri Lanka, 2003. Milinda Moragoda, Minister for Science and Economic Reform, addresses an ICF seminar jointly led by Sir Mark Tully (Left) and me.

His concluding remarks were a rallying call: 'I have no need to ask for an apology from anybody. So many people suffered more horrifically than I did. But there is a need for the truth to be told, so that innocent people on all sides can reach out their hands and live as neighbours in tolerance and respect. We used to live like that in our city of four religions. That is the Bosnia that I would like to experience again.'

In these days of suspicion and hostility between Islam and the rest of the world, it is worth recording that more than half of the participants in the assembly were Moslems. There is no barrier between men and women of goodwill who are working to build a better future.

Women were a major force at Sarajevo: Senator Jara Moserova of the Czech Parliament; Jolanta Kwasniewska, First Lady of Poland; Ellen Hume, a leading USA journalist; Faustina Starrett, journalist and media lecturer from Derry in Northern Ireland with her experience of emerging hope from years of conflict; Choice Okoro, a brilliant young Nigerian tabloid journalist; Natalya Skvortsova, President of the Journalists' Union in Russia's third city of Nizhny Novgorod; Elivira Begović, organiser of the Assembly, later becoming Bosnia's Ambassador to the United Kingdom; Apolline de Malherbe from Paris. Three of the ICF's six Vice-Presidents are women. I had invited my granddaughter, Natalie, to the assembly, so that she might know something of her ancestral roots.

One of the people whose vision lay behind the congress was Senad Kamenica, responsible for news programmes on Bosnian Television. He came from a Moslem background, had been wounded and captured during the fighting and, when the war ended, had tried to play a positive role. His courageous action in broadcast reporting had prevented the multi-ethnic schools from being split up into ethnic schools. He still believed in the traditional values of his city. And his vision for the congress was that 'Sarajevo, which had been a city of shame for the

20th century, could become a beacon of hope for the 21st'. He has been working with the Baltic Media Centre concerned with the development of news programmes and documentaries throughout South East Europe.

Since my stay in the late fifties I have been back to India several times on media missions. On one occasion I was a delegate to the four-yearly Congress of the International Publishers Association in New Delhi. The Dalai Lama was a guest speaker and I always remember him telling us that we would be in better health ourselves if we looked after the well-being of our employees more diligently – an interesting cause and effect case. Could it be universally true for all boss/worker relationships? Anyway it made me think and act accordingly, and I have no reason to dispute it.

At that time Rajmohan Gandhi, a grandson of the Mahatma and, on his mother's side, of Rajagopalachari, the first Governor General of independent India, was a Member of the Raj Sabha, the country's Upper House of Parliament. He was a journalist by profession, having trained on *The Scotsman,* and had later become editor of the Madras edition of the *Indian Express*, a leading English-language newspaper. He believed in, lived out and promoted the basic ideas of the Mahatma and I had asked him to be part of the International Communications Forum (ICF). He became a member of its Advisory Council.

We decided to invite some of the Publishers' Congress participants to his MP's bungalow to meet a group of New Delhi media people and to discuss the role of the media as a constructive force in society. It was an enthralling evening in a crowded room with many sitting on the floor and a very lively debate ensued. The next morning a leading publisher told me that it had been the highlight of his visit.

In March 2003 I spent five days in Nagaland, a semi-autonomous area of North East India, at the invitation of the Centre for Democracy and Tribal Studies in Kohima, the state capital. It is a state of some nine million inhabitants bordering on Myanmar (formerly Burma), with more than 50 tribal groups (somewhat akin to Scottish clans), with such a variety of unwritten tongues that, by necessity, English is the official language. It seems strange, in this beautiful mountainous area, that all the signs, shop names and the newspapers are in the foreign language of English. Once part of the British Empire, its citizens played a heroic role in halting the Japanese advance into India during World War II.

My programme was arranged by Charles Chasie, a writer and journalist who had taken part in the ICF events in Russia and Bosnia. He is active in promoting unity between the tribes and in developing their relations with India and the wider world. He had asked me to be the godfather to his 18-month old son, Mhiaphovi, and a great family reunion was held to mark the occasion.

During the visit I met with the Governor, Shyamel Dutts, a former Head of Indian Intelligence Services; R S Pandey, the Chief Secretary of the State; heads of several government departments and leaders of the churches (Nagaland is largely Christian with strong Baptist and Catholic influences); teachers and other professional groups. I spoke at public meetings, took part in a presentation by youth leaders and met with the press and broadcasters.

I visited the Kohima War Cemetery, where hundreds of British, Indian and Naga soldiers lie. My visit to Kohima took place as the results of a state election were coming through, followed by the horse-trading for the formation of a new coalition government. Many of the new Members of the Legislative Assembly were staying in the same hotel, and security was at its height. It was the first time that I had stayed at a hotel with an armed soldier outside my window.

On a deeper level I experienced the love-hate relationship that the Naga people have for the British. On the one hand an older man thanked me that the British had brought Nagaland from the Middle Ages to our modern society without distress and revolution. But another said that Britain had let them down in not standing for their independence as a nation. They had wanted to be a free and united country, but were absorbed into independent India. There were still five, armed, underground groups who resisted the Indian presence. People like Chasie are working to solve tensions and to find the way to reconciliation.

In its manifesto, the Centre for Democracy and Tribal Studies states: 'The Centre believes that peaceful methods are better than violence, that transparent discussion is more fruitful than coercion and intolerance, and that all problems can be worked out through reasoned arguments and truthful dialogue.' Speaking at a meeting organised by the Centre, I said: 'You may feel that Nagaland needs the help of the world, and it is true that we should give it. But I would also like to say that the world needs Nagaland, a land that will have worked out the answers to internal conflicts and to those with its neighbours and, by so demonstrating reconciliation and progress to humanity, will bring hope and inspiration to the troubled areas of the planet.'

*   *   *   *   *   *   *

During the last decade of the 20th century a sea change took place in media attitudes. From being rather indifferent towards public opinion over criticism of their ethical standards or lack of them, the media steadily became more self-critical in the light of declining public confidence.

In polls related to the trust of the public in various business and professional activities it hit very low scores. In an Australian poll in 1997, it achieved only seven per cent, with politicians just nosing ahead with eight per cent. The only activity below them was second-hand car dealing.

One practical consequence in the USA was the emergence of the Committee of Concerned Journalists which aimed to resist the idea of 'infotainment' and 'If it bleeds, it leads' in news presentation. Bill Kovach, then Curator of Harvard's Nieman Foundation, was one of its principal instigators.

The ICF felt that it was well placed to help restore public confidence and for this purpose held a major place in its end-of-the-decade events. A one-day conference on this theme was hosted by *The Financial Times*, its Chairman David Bell, and other sponsors in early 1999. It was attended by more than 100 of Britain's media leaders, including eight national editors, top columnists and senior people in television and the radio. An international element was added by leading figures from Australia, France and the USA. Lord Nolan, the law Lord, who had headed the British Government's Committee on Standards in Public Life, chaired the conference. He summed up the ideals for creating public goodwill as 'honesty, openness, accountability, integrity, leadership and selflessness'. 'To achieve this,' he added 'courage was a very necessary quality for journalists, as well as humour, humility and a sense of proportion.'

Even as I write I see in a current issue of *The Times* that media professionals are among those who 'lie at the bottom of the workplace happiness league table drawn up by the City and Guilds Training Board'. It is hard to stomach that journalists are among the most unhappy and least trusted people in British society. How do the owners of the media and the leaders of professional associations react to this? Do they continue to keep digging in the hole they are in or are they seriously seeking for the way to climb out?

The conference at the *Financial Times* marked a significant step forward in our appraisal of our role in society. There have been hopeful developments, some of which have grown out of the actions of people at the FT event. The ICF was represented at an informal consultation initiated by Sheila Bloom, Director of the UK Trust of the Institute of Global Ethics, at St George's House, Windsor Castle, in December 2002. The subject was the desirability of establishing a Centre for Media Affairs. It was chaired by Lord McNally and attended by several media associations and charitable bodies.

An Interim Advisory Group was formed which organised a further meeting held at the Guardian and Observer Visitor Centre in London, on 'Journalism and Media Ethics in a Democracy'. A steering group was created, chaired by David Kingsley, which included Robin Williamson, Executive Director of the ICF, and Mike Jempson, Director of the Presswise Trust, a UK charity.

Presswise changed its name to Mediawise and sought substantial financial support. Donations were received from the Esmee Fairbairn Foundation and the Joseph Rowntree Charitable Trust to underwrite the appointment of a Development Director and cover two years' running costs.

In 2004 Mediawise issued a Declaration of Intent for the development of the Centre for Media Affairs:

- Our belief is that in an open and democratic society there needs to be a relationship of mutual trust and responsibility between media and civil society.

- Our role is to generate dialogue in order to develop and maintain trust between media professionals and the public.

- We will be a place where media professionals and the general public can bring their concerns on ethical issues in the media and find a source of guidance and training.

- We expect to be measured by the media and public on the basis of whether we add value to debate, challenge practices and attitudes among organisations and individuals and achieve changes for the better. We will also judge our success by the extent to which our work and activities are disseminated by the media and supported by the public.

The ICF, through Robin Williamson, remains closely associated with the Centre and we shall evaluate and support the contributions it makes to bring about a competent and trustworthy media scene in Britain. I hope it will create a model that will inspire similar activities worldwide.

* * * * * * *

As I complete this book I am in my 85th year. When it comes to driving a car I am still in my twenties, when it comes to running my life I am still in my forties and when it comes to being concerned about the world situation I am still in my sixties.

For all that there is still to achieve, I believe that the last 15 years of my life have been the most satisfying and effective. I could ask myself the question why I did not make better use of my younger years. I know that one reason is that I was strongly locked into making money and achieving success. Your family life becomes secondary, and you are not effectively confronting the social and ethical problems of society.

I am always encouraged when friends say to me that it is not what you know that has been done by the International Communications Forum but what you don't know that is significant. Nevertheless, I have never been able to be satisfied with what we have achieved, because there is always so much more to be done. Fortunately this state of affairs deflates natural vanity and dents unmerited pride.

I hope that we have started a current in the media world of the 21st century that will enable this talented and persevering body of men and women to fulfil their role of service and inspiration to a bewildered and dysfunctional humanity.

Afterword

By Bernard Margueritte, President of the International Communications Forum and correspondent for the French media in Warsaw

Here I was in the Cambridge, Massachusetts, home of Ann and Bryan Hamlin, meeting their guest Bill Porter for the first time. Me, a pretty typical Frenchman facing somebody who is as British as one can be and yet, against all the odds, I immediately felt on the same wave-length, with the same approach to problems.

The timing was good. I was at that time a Fellow at nearby Harvard University and shocked to be there, in the country of The First Amendment, hearing every week the complaints of the best American journalists like Ted Koppel or Johnny Apple Jr. They were telling us that this is the end of our trade, that we should be ashamed of what we were doing. I was in the right mood to get acquainted with Bill Porter's message.

Bill writes a lot in his book about destiny. And certainly destiny, or the hand of God, was there from the very beginning. Mike Lowe, a teacher of our son in Warsaw, first put me in touch with the Hamlins and then Caux. MRA, now Initiatives of Change, gave me a proper perspective on what Bill Porter – and all of us in the ICF – want to do with the media.

My fight for the dignity of the media had to start with myself, with my constant failures to live according to my moral and spiritual principles. This is a huge debt I, for one, owe to Bill Porter.

169

Bill found his mission in this world pretty late in life. What an example! What a source of permanent hope! The story is never told until the end. It is never too late. Jean-Paul Sartre, to quote an improbable source, said that you cannot make a judgment on anyone until his or her last day, since to the last minute everyone has the chance to find him/herself.

Will the ICF, will the spirit of Bill Porter prevail? One thing is certain: we will continue the battle. 'If not us, then who? If not now, then when?' Bill is an exceptional man, one of those few charismatic people, who can inspire and lead. Bill can speak about values and ethical goals in a way that, in someone else's mouth, would only provoke a condescending smile and be regarded as wishy-washy, empty preaching. And yet he touches the heart and mind of people. Everyone feels that this man is genuine, that he is simply telling the truth.

And the truth is that it is high time for us people in the media to reflect on what we do. For our own sake but also for the sake of the world, since what we do has such a great impact on society. The goals are clear. In every country we must serve the citizens with honesty, truth and openness and give them all they need to make up their own minds. This is the only way to promote and preserve a living democracy. It is no small task. And then in our foreign reporting, we must inform about 'the other', with generosity, so that we can move from information to understanding and from there to mutual understanding and respect.

Bill is still the youngest and most enthusiastic among us. I feel I have been blessed to meet him, and I pledge to do my best to continue his mission. We will always hear the clear sound of his trumpet calling us to the battle.

Appendix I

'Finding a purpose for life'

A dialogue between Bill Porter and his granddaughter,
Natalie, at a Caux conference in 1999

Natalie: Grandpa, suddenly at the age of 70 you found a
           great purpose for your life and you have been
           getting younger ever since. What happened?

Bill: And you, at the age of twenty realised that you
           needed a purpose. What happened then?

Natalie: You go first.

Bill: You must have been observing me through curious
           eyes from time to time. In your childhood I was a
           very busy publishing executive with little time for
           family diversions. You probably saw me on rare
           occasions at your parents' house for a meal or out
           at my country home in the west of England. You
           always tried to help me in the garden, which was a
           great test of my patience. All the time I was rising
           in the publishing world and taking on responsibili-
           ties with its associations. Then your granny and I
           went to live in France at the seaside resort of Le
           Touquet and you and your mum came over there
           once or twice. It was there that I started to think
           through where the media could become a positive
           force in society and the implications of that. Then
           your granny died and occasionally I would meet
           you in London and take you out for dinner. I must
           have talked sometimes about my new thinking.

171

Were you aware of these phases in my life and what did you make of them?

Natalie: You spoke very often of your new thinking and I have very mixed ideas and feelings on the new and ever-changing grandpa you were becoming. Each time I saw you, the more you changed. It was strange though because it was at a time that I was very lost within myself, so I both admired your new-found purpose but at the same time I resented it. Everything you would tell me was so admirable Grandpa; you were following your senses and acting on them, you were spreading a good and positive message, you were reaching out of your world and thinking of others, where I was stuck in my world, and my world was not a happy one as a rebellious teenager. The good in people was a threat in my world because deep down it was what I wanted for my own life, but I was struggling with my identity and MY sense of purpose was a big blur. But I knew I'd get there one day.

Bill: It's good to know all that.

Natalie: Why did you take an interest in me at all times and keep faith in me, even during my most rebellious years?

Bill: Firstly it is natural for persons to love their grand-children. You get affection without responsibility for one thing. But most of all I saw in you the spark of your remarkable granny and also your own unique possibility of being a force for good in a rough world.

Natalie: But what could you do about that to get me on the right track?

Bill: Well, I knew at the time of your interest in dance
          and acting, so I invited you to spend time at the
          Caux Conference Centre in Switzerland with its
          theatre and arts groups. Eventually I think that I
          must have sponsored you to take part in that three
          times. How did those experiences grab you?

Natalie: My first experience was quite an unusual one. At
          first I was in complete awe of the setting and I had
          this feeling deep inside that I had come somewhere
          really good. But I wasn't ready for the content of
          Caux and so I took it all with a pinch of salt. I
          rebelled against a lot of the ideas and rules but I
          don't think this was because I didn't agree with the
          ideas; it was more a fear of what I may find if I
          examined myself too closely. I chose to ignore the
          challenges and I was left feeling quite angry that
          you had sent me there for over a month to fend for
          myself. I didn't, at the age of seventeen, want to
          examine my integrity. Yet, when you asked me the
          following year if I'd like to go back I found I said
          yes without any thought. Something pulled me
          back; it was the good in me connecting with the
          good feelings I felt when I first went there. And I
          am glad I returned. Did you ever lose faith in me?

Bill: No, I realised that you were going through a lot of
          suffering from the break-up of your parents' marriage
          and that you had been thrown too much onto your
          own devices. But I also knew from my own experi-
          ence that the sins and shortcomings of others were no
          excuse for mine, and I felt that you had the strength
          of personality to face up to that yourself.

Natalie: We'll come back to that, but could we talk about
          Granny, your wife, whom I truly admired,

especially as she always talked straight to me, with plenty of humour.

Bill: I think that she was incapable of not saying what she thought, which was very good for an Englishman who would rather say nothing than speak his mind. She was totally sincere, although I did sometimes dispute with her that sincerity was not necessarily the truth. Anyway I believe that because of her I became much more open with myself. Her last gift to me, less than four weeks before she died was to enable me to find some purpose for the rest of my life.

Natalie: I'm the same age now that she was when she was condemned to death in the Second World War. Life in London has never been like that. She must have had a sense of purpose to have got through all that. It must have been a love of country and, perhaps, a sense of unknown destiny.

Bill: She was certainly a woman of great resilience and panache and, when I met her later, it must have been these qualities that caused me to fall in love and end my bachelordom. Well, she was also a good-looking redhead and I always had a weakness for red hair. What do you remember most about her?

Natalie: I remember her tremendous strength of character. I felt a strong love and commitment to her country and her heritage. I also felt a lot of hurt and pain connected to her past, but I never got the feeling she was running away from the past. She was afraid of very little, always spoke her mind very clearly and matter-of-factly. When I was a young girl I used to find her frankness embarrassing. I would cringe when I heard her speak to some

people, but as I got older I understood that
honesty is imperative and if something is said that
is not said to hurt anyone, well, then I think it's
great to be honest and express what it is that's in
your heart.

Bill: Do you think that women have a special purpose?

Natalie: Like what?

Bill: Like improving men, which would seem a lifetime
of work rarely, if ever, taken through to women's
complete satisfaction!

Natalie: You are joking. There is more to it than that. But
did Granny improve you?

Bill: Surely. But she did more than that. She helped me
to find out what was my destiny and what I was
supposed to be doing in this life that would build a
better future for everyone. From that time I found
an inner compulsion to strive for the media to
become a constructive force in the life of humanity,
and it has never left me to this day. My wife was
to die soon after our talk, but she had set me on
the road that was to be the finest part of my life.

Natalie: You mentioned inner compulsion. What does that
mean?

Bill: It must be a major factor in having an effective
purpose. Some think that it is the spirit of God
working in a person's heart and mind. I often
describe myself as a lapsed agnostic, because this
experience has given me a sense of faith, which had
long ago deserted me. I believe it is possible for
each one of us to find his or her sense of destiny.
Conscience plays a big role. I had to look squarely

at, and put right, the moral compromises in my life. To be specific, in my business life I had passed company accounts that I knew to be inaccurate, had sanctioned promotion campaigns that I knew to be deceptive and had defended policies that I knew were not in the best interests of our employees and customers. That had to end. As you peel off the often deeply encrusted layers of wrong doing, you get a greater sense of reality and purpose and become a human being whose life matters. I strongly recommend this process to all. Now I would like you to tell me the real turning points in your life.

Natalie: Do you remember the dinner that we had in 1997? I was in tears because of the breach between my father and me. We had not even spoken to each other for two years or more. But then I told you, 'I have realised that I have two needs in my life, one is a spiritual base and the other is a purpose, and I have neither.'

Bill: To me that was an amazing moment. That, at 21 years of age, you had already realised that.

Natalie: Yes, but for me the problem was how to find them. I had been told of a leadership-training course in Australia that had helped some of the girls whom I had met. I decided to apply for it, feeling that at least some time out of the superficial life of West London could do nothing but good.

Bill: I was very supportive of this and had a meeting with your dad. I asked him why he was not seeing you. He said it was because you were very unreliable. I said 'Look who's talking! At her age you were a world champion unreliable person and now

you see it in your daughter and you don't like it.'
Something must have stirred in him because he
went to see you before you went to Australia.
Anyway, what happened?

Natalie: Well, first and foremost I had to be really honest
about just where I was at within myself, and the
truth was I was in a very ugly place inside. I had
used drugs and alcohol in my life for a number of
years. I had become an addict, which meant I had
lost control of my true identity. I reacted to life in a
false way, I hid my emotions behind alcoholism
and appeared to be having fun, but that was only
because the drugs dictated who I was. The reality
was that I was a very lost and unhappy young lady.

So when I got to Australia I made a positive
decision to eradicate all substances from my life
and find an alternative. And this decision was to
be my saving grace. This decision led to an
unfolding process that was to be the beginning of
my life the way it was meant to be, the way God
intended. Often when we are ashamed of something we have done in our lives we try to hide it
and push it away in the past, but instead of doing
this I confronted it all and realised what I needed
to do was forgive myself and be honest with
myself about the past. Once I realised the pain of
the past, I suddenly found I could focus on the
future and at this point the future no longer
seemed so uninviting. Silent times for me in the
past had been too fearful, for I was afraid of what
I might hear or rather I wouldn't hear and just
that deadly silence. Spiritually you could say I was
dead. But once I had begun the healing process in
me, I found a spiritual awakening and found a

friend in God that was to remain with me and be my guidance and help me find my purpose.

One day, while I was in Australia, I went to Adelaide and a small group of us visited a home for young aboriginal teenagers who were seen as 'troublemakers' in society because they used alcohol and drugs. I really empathised with these young people and felt a real connection with them. I felt really positive though, because I had seen the dramatic change within myself and so knew it was possible for them also. I suddenly felt a belonging in my life. It occurred to me that all the experiences I had had were meant for a reason and that was to help others. My insight into their world could be a friendly hand to help them out of theirs. So my past became my key to a meaningful purpose in life.

Bill: And what has replaced those addictions?

Natalie: In recovery I'm learning a new behaviour, it's called being who I am. For me this was very frightening. What would happen if I felt what I felt, said what I wanted, became firm about my beliefs and valued what I needed? What would happen if I let go of my camouflage, what would happen if I owned my power to be myself? Would people still like me? Would they go away? There comes a time when we become willing and ready to take that risk. To continue growing and living with ourselves we realise we must liberate ourselves. It's time to stop allowing ourselves to be controlled by others and their expectations and be true to ourselves. This is what I did. Some people did depart from my life but I realise those relationships would have ended anyway. Some stayed and lived and respected me more for taking the risk of being who I am. I have discovered that who I am has always been good enough, because it was who I was intended to be. And finally Grandpa, how do you sum up your experience of purpose?

Bill: I suppose I always had a motivation of some kind. Like staying alive during the war, like a few years of idealism when peace began, when many of us wanted to feel our comrades had not died in vain, and in Britain we voted in a socialist government that created the so-called 'welfare state' in the hope of ending poverty and unemployment. But then I was overtaken by the desire for security and success in my business and publishing life. And then I had a wife and your dad to support. Eventually, I reached a point at which I had enough money not to need to ask how much something would cost, but only if I wanted it. Your granny was one of the best-dressed women in London and my career was forever making progress. But millions were dying of starvation in Africa and elsewhere, violence was on the increase in our western cities and schools, and the United Nations said that ethnic conflict was actual or potential in a thousand flashpoints around the world.

Well I have told you what happened to me then. I did find an enduring and inspiring purpose, and I believe this can happen to everyone with an open heart to receive it.

Appendix II

The Battleline of Civilisation

This essay was written by William Porter, for the World Association of Newspapers, and appeared as a Guest Column on their web site and is reproduced with WAN's permission. The opinions expressed are those of the author and do not necessarily reflect those of the World Association of Newspapers.

Those of us who work in the media did not come from another planet to report on the dying days of the Earth's civilisation and then to return from whence we came. We are part of this society with children, grandchildren and loved ones for whom we would like to see a more secure and fairer world.

The Earth's population seems to consist of two groups, the concerned and the indifferent. It is probable that within the ranks of media professionals there is a big percentage of the concerned. Many came into it with a sense of idealism and others developed a high degree of social responsibility as they reacted to the needs and shortcomings of the people whom they were meeting. A few acquired a hardened cynicism that tainted their colleagues and corrupted their audiences.

What is the role of this privileged and intelligent group of humanity in what Samuel Huntington has described as 'the clash of civilisations' and in what he goes on to call 'the remaking of world order'? In the context of my essay it is important to understand what is meant by 'Civilisation'. It is not just Western culture rising from the Greco-Roman and Judaeo-Christian traditions, although they are an important

180

part of it. It is the sum total of the strivings of humankind to find stability, purpose and satisfaction through the emergence of faiths and structures and systems that enable its creative and social aspirations to be achieved. It is rooted in the cultures and religions of Asia and the Arab World. It owes much to the customs and spirituality of the tribes and villagers of Africa, the Americas and Australasia. All these sources add up to Civilisation with a big C. It has never achieved its objectives in totality and it is constantly under threat. That it should achieve those objectives and overcome those threats is the prime purpose and destiny of human life.

Unfortunately, one of the greatest dangers to this Civilisation is the conflict between the smaller civilisations, often religions, ethnic groups and national and regional cultures. The other, subtler danger is the greed and ambition of men and women, often manifested through political ideologies, selfish capitalism, the struggle for market domination and international crime.

Rajmohan Gandhi, newspaperman and a grandson of the Mahatma, said, 'Class hate as an ideology is behind us. But ethnic hate is with us and ahead of us. Who will now expose the illogicality of ethnic enmity? Who will disentangle the love of one's own people, which is a great quality, from disliking of another people? Who will report and interpret reconciliation and forgiveness? Ethnic enmity wins applause and votes and prime ministerships. Many so-called patriots or nationalists say that you cannot love your own people unless you hate other people. It is an obvious folly. Part of the role of communications is to unseat this folly from the minds and hearts of the millions of the world.'

Vaclev Havel, surely one of our best political thinkers of today, wrote, 'I think that there are good reasons for suggesting that the modern age has ended. Today many things indicate that we are going through a transitional period, when it seems that something is on the way out and something else is painfully being born. It is as if something were crumbling, decaying, and exhausting itself, while something else, still indistinct, were arising from the rubble.'

Much earlier the Canadian statesman, Lester Pearson, said, 'The future of both peace and civilisation depend upon understanding and co-operation among the political, spiritual and intellectual forces of the world's major civilisations. In the greater, global "real clash" between Civilisation and barbarism, the world's civilisations with their rich accomplishments in religion, art, literature and philosophy, science, technology, morality and compassion will hang together or hang separately.'

If these assessments are true, and I believe that they are, then the media should be interpreting them to their audiences. A leading, world-level, woman business leader, interviewed on BBC World Radio, said, doubtless under some provocation, 'Most journalists cannot tell the difference of significance between a bicycle accident and the decline of Civilisation'.

Professor Grigory Pomerans, one of Russia's few respected philosophers of today, is convinced that our present bevy of civilisations are in decline and that we have to create a new Civilisation. Personally, I am not sure whether we are in the business of saving a Civilisation or creating a new one. No matter which way, this is the great news story of the millennium, if we have the wit and the prescience to see it.

I am now going to make the comparison of the situation in time of conventional war, when we know who is fighting who and where are the lines of conflict. Today we are concerned with what can be called the Battle Line of Civilisation in which the adversaries are the constructive and the destructive forces at work in the world. There are those striving for good and those who consciously or unknowingly promote evil. Those who are architects and builders and those who are destroyers and underminers. And where are the lines of conflict? Huntington talks about the 'fault lines' between religions and national interests and historical legacies. They also run through the hearts and mind of all men and women whenever they are faced with a moral choice.

There is always excitement in war situations. But now we have a situation of even greater excitement, in which we can be reporting and interpreting all news in relation to the destiny of humanity. We would have to ask ourselves the question about all hard news. Is what is happening contributing to the undermining of Civilisation or to the building of a new and just society? Every government action, every multinational company decision, every new book or film, every television programme, every environmental issue could be assessed for their relevance to this basic confrontation.

It should be possible to introduce this element of confrontation and of effort, ground lost or gained, into modern news writing and broadcasting. How can we define this supreme conflict of our time? 'Once to every man and nation comes the moment to decide, in the fight twixt truth and falsehood, for the good or evil side.' Every journalist will understand that. But it can be further defined as between freedom and bondage, between fairness and injustice, between peace and war, between honesty and lies, between caring and indifference, between wholesomeness and decadence, between family unity and breakdown, between ... the list could go on, and most of us know darned well the right choice to make. In each case a line is drawn on either side of which victory or defeat can be signalled.

Walter Cronkite, the great American newsman, wrote in the concluding chapter of his autobiography, *A Reporter's Life*, 'The new technologies give proof of the human being's intellectual capacity. Can we really believe that we are incapable of applying that same intellectual power to solving the great problems the world faces, overpopulation, pollution and poverty chief among them?

'Can we believe that the beleaguered peoples of the world

will long be tolerant of those who possess the tools, but who can't make them work for the good of humankind everywhere?'

'There is going to be social and political and economic revolution, which will explode with such suddenness as to have the character of revolution. The revolutionary forces are already at work today, and they have humankind's dream on their side. We (the media) don't want to be on the other side. It is up to us to assume leadership of that revolution, to channel it in a direction that will ensure freedom's future', Cronkite concluded.

The back-up of the media to this challenge is to inform, thoroughly and with balance, our audiences of what is happening in their localities, communities, nations, regions and the world; to encourage and help them to cope with the situation, as it realistically exists; and to work with them for the good to triumph. This concept does not mean the imposition of morality or belief or dogma, but rather an honest presentation of the battle and its issues, plus an encouragement to participate and a pointing of ways in building a better society. Each individual in an audience is free to form his or her opinion and to take or not to take any action that might be indicated. There will always be an indifferent majority, but the future will belong to a motivated, creative minority.

I am thinking here of bringing an element of purpose and excitement into the whole field of news and current affairs reporting and presentation. Of course there are some areas that will not lend themselves to this type of treatment, and they should be handled in accordance with traditional practice. This is also true in times of war, when not all news is related to the conflict. A big problem with most news treatment today is that it is without any context other than its effect on circulation and audience size, and I am not underestimating the importance of that, but, even then, it needs some kind of yardstick against which to make judgments.

How is news value estimated today? At its worst by the blood and guts on the floor. At its best by its human appeal, and even that, usually on a sentimental basis, as with Princess Diana, the Woodward case or the behavioural idiosyncrasies of celebrities.

In the recent prominence given to attacks on refugees in prosperous western countries there was the cry of appeal from a Glasgow housewife, 'I wish the media would listen to the decent people, the ordinary people, who so care about the suffering of others'.

I think that most of my colleagues in the media will understand what I am getting at, in spite of my struggles to express it. And the concept of a Battle Line of Civilisation gives us a reasonable and purposeful basis on which to work. From 'If it bleeds, it leads' to 'If it answers needs, it leads' may seem a long way off, but I believe that it is a road we have to take.

THE SARAJEVO COMMITMENT

At the beginning of the 21st century men and women of the media register their commitment to integrity and public service.
This document was launched at a World Media Assembly,
SARAJEVO 2000, and signed by participants on 30 September 2000.

We, men and women of the media – professionals at all levels, from publishers and producers to cub reporters and students of journalism; from the print and digital media, television and radio, book publishing, cinema and theatre, advertising and public relations, music and the performing and creative arts – met here in the bruised, historic and beautiful city of Sarajevo, to pay our homage and respect to the millions of humanity whom we inform, entertain and educate.

We look back on a century of brilliance and bloodshed, of amazing technological advance and distressing human misery, of mobility and isolation and of healing and hatred. A century in which two world wars emanated from the so-called advanced and civilised continent of Europe. A century in which we split the atom, but left families, communities and nations divided. A century which ended with some 30 unresolved major conflict situations.

We accept that we in the media, whilst talent and technology enabled us to reach the lives of almost every last person in the world, were not able to create the climate in which problems were solved, conflicting groups and interests reconciled, and peace and justice established.

Now that we confront a new century, many of us, hoping that we interpret the views and feelings of the vast majority of our colleagues, would like to establish a commitment, an undertaking, a pledge, to all those who will live and love and work in these coming hundred years.

We shall inform you to the best of our ability, with clarity and honesty, with independence of mind, of what is truly happening in the world at the level of the individual, the family, the community, the nation and the region. We shall present the facts and explain the facts, and some of us will aim with modesty to interpret them. As we succeed in doing this, we believe that you, the people, will be enabled to make the right decisions, to elect and appoint the best leaders and to build a fair, just and compassionate society.

We seek a world in which everyone cares enough and everyone shares enough so that everyone will have enough; a world in which the work and wealth of the world are available to all at the exploitation of none.

We shall provide the art and entertainment which will inspire, arouse and give hope and a sense of direction to all humanity.

We shall be working to raise up and not to drag down. We shall challenge our politicians to work for the next generation and not the next election, encourage our governments to make agreements which are effective in people's hearts as well as on paper; and stimulate our business, industrial and labour leaders to meet the material needs of humankind with fairness and equity.

We shall work to educate, through all the means of communication, generations who will be able to confront the challenges of their age with competence and vision.

We shall combine freedom with responsibility, talent with humility, privilege with service, comfort with sacrifice and concern with courage. We realise that change in society begins with change in ourselves.

We undertake to apply and demonstrate in our own lives the values that we hope for, and often demand, in others. We shall confront hypocrisy, oppression, exploitation and evil, firstly by our own clarity and straightness and then through the means by which we reach our audiences. We are unlikely to be perfect, but we shall aim to be truthful and free of guile, selfish ambition, perverted behaviour and deception.

We shall not cease to strive until every gun is silent, every injustice righted and every human being enabled to live a life of satisfaction and purpose.

To all these intentions and obligations, we commit ourselves at this time of beginning. May the higher aspirations within us all, be they spiritual, moral or humanistic, enable us to fulfil this commitment.

Index

192

Photo credits

Photo No:
6.   Council of Europe
8.   Jeremy McCabe
11. © Liz Garnett, 29 Belgrave Court, London SW8
18.   Hannen Foss
23. Arthur Strong
30. © L'Osservatore Romano, 00120 Citta del Vaticano
34. Aberdeen City Council, Publicity and Promotion Unit

   Other photos by David Channer, Hugh Nowell, Jean-Jacques Odier,
   Christoph Spreng